CD-ROM
Applications
and Markets

Supplements to
Optical Information Systems

CD-ROM
Applications
and Markets

edited by
JUDITH PARIS ROTH

Meckler
WESTPORT · LONDON

Supplement to *Optical Information Systems,* no. 3

Library of Congress Cataloging-in-Publication Data

CD-ROM applications and markets / edited by Judith Paris Roth.
    p.   cm. -- (Supplement to optical information systems ; 3)
    Bibliography: p.
    Includes index.
    ISBN 0-88736-332-6 (alk. paper)
    1. CD-ROM industry--United States. 2. Market surveys--United
States. I. Roth, Judith Paris. II. Series.
HD9696.0673U6265 1988

381' .4500456--dc19   88-13350
                                                      CIP

British Library Cataloguing in Publication Data

CD-ROM applications and markets.
    1. Computer systems. Read only memory :
    Compact discs
    I. Roth, Judith Paris
    004.5'6

    ISBN 0-88736-332-6

Meckler Corporation, 11 Ferry Lane West, Westport, CT 06880.
Meckler Ltd., Grosvenor Gardens House, Grosvenor Gardens,
    London SW1W 0BS, U.K.

Printed on acid free paper.
Manufactured in the United States of America.

Contents

Preface

This book provides the reader with a look at the major application and product trends in the library, medical/scientific, government and legal, business and retail, and education markets in the United States. Rather than an accounting of every application, actual and under development, as well as every product now available on the market, this book concentrates on representative applications and products that highlight current trends in product and market development. It does not attempt to catalog every CD-ROM application and/or product, but by shedding some light on current trends, the goal is to influence future directions concerning the implementation and utilization of the technology.

Each chapter describes applications in terms of product and/or market development. Rather than describing each application currently on the market today, authors focus on major trends in products and applications available in a specific market. Application and market areas addressed in this book are library and information services, medical/health care and science, government and law, and education. It concludes with a chapter on CD-ROM marketing strategies as well as current and future trends.

Each chapter includes a directory of names and addresses of firms offering products and services in a particular marketplace. Specifically, *CD-ROM Applications and Markets* is divided into the following chapters.

Chapter 1. The author, a librarian who has been following the CD-ROM field since 1985, examines current trends in CD-ROM application and product offerings for the library and information service sector.

Chapter 2. The author describes the various trends in current applications of CD-ROM technology in the medical/health care and scientific markets. Comfortable with the utilization and incorporation of high technology into their everyday work lives as well as demonstrating a strong need to stay abreast of scientific developments, the medical and scientific marketplace offers great promise to CD-ROM product and application developers.

Chapter 3. Government and law applications and their markets are the focus of this chapter. Government agencies as well as private firms are pursuing new markets using CD-ROM technology. The author speculates on the hurdles confronting product and application developers interested in penetrating the legal market.

Chapter 4. While the education market has yet to be targeted by many firms offering CD-ROM products and services, there are a variety of products testing the market's acceptance of this technology. The author describes the barriers to the educational market's acceptance of CD-ROM technology and offers a set of recommendations to product and application developers interested in entering this market.

Chapter 5. Written by an experienced CD-ROM application and product developer, this chapter examines current business and retail marketing strategies and future trends affecting the expansion of CD-ROM business opportunities in the 1980s and 1990s.

An *Appendix* briefly describes CD-ROM technology and standards references and *Information Resources* is a list of recommended reading sources for further information.

Naturally, throughout the book, discussion of a product or company should not be considered an endorsement and does not imply its superiority over competing applications, products, or systems.

My appreciation goes to both Ann Stapleton for her thorough, efficient, and competent editing, and Tony Abbott for his continued excellent editorial support. My gratitude to Alan Meckler for his continued commitment to optical information technologies. Lastly, this book would not be a reality without the ever-present support and encouragement of my husband, Bryan, for whom I have the highest regard.

Judith Paris Roth
July 1988

Introduction

C ompact disc has been the fastest growth technology for both the entertainment and computer storage industries. In less than four short years, CD-ROM has made its presence known in the library and medical/scientific markets. Within the next few years, CD-ROM is expected to become a powerful tool for information retrieval, storage, and access in such established markets as business and legal information, science and medicine, library reference, and education. Desktop publishing and presentation graphics, software distribution, and multimedia applications for home and business are just a few of the newest markets for which CD-ROM products are now being developed.

According to manufacturer and product developers, there will be at least 50,000 CD-ROM drives in the marketplace by the end of 1988. An undetermined number of these drives are test units for organizations and companies considering using the technology. There are now several authoritative print directories of CD-ROM applications that describe a vast and diverse array of actual applications of CD-ROM technology in both the private and public sectors. These applications include technical documentation support, multimedia encyclopedias, indexes, computer software, scientific and reference data, bibliographic databases, and new business information products.

Market research firms and technology analysts expect that CD-ROM technology will be a multi-billion dollar industry by the early 1990s. The creation of basic standards for information interchange have served to foster the growth and development of CD-ROM technology to a great extent.

Since CD-ROM's introduction, many information providers, hardware vendors, and software developers have decried the absence of both national and international standards. It was strongly believed by many industry experts that without standards, customer acceptance, use, and application of the technology would be difficult to achieve. The International Standards Organization (ISO) 9660 Volume and File Structure of CD-ROM Information Interchange (IS 9660 CD-ROM Standard) is a single international CD-ROM standard. ISO 9660 allows use of information processing systems in conformance with ISO 9660 to mount and read any ISO 9660-conformant CD-ROM discs. The establishment of basic standards for CD-ROM technology has helped to build a strong interest in CD-ROM in a diverse range of markets.

An example of the kind of market development expected in the near term is reflected in the joint DEC-Apple-Microsoft announcement made at the March 1988 Microsoft Third Annual International Conference on CD-ROM. Apple Computer, Inc., Digital Equipment Corporation, and Microsoft Corporation plan to support the ISO 9660 CD-ROM Standard. The standard is expected to allow information providers to create a single master CD-ROM disc that will be read by Digital Equipment Corporation's VAX family of computers, industry standard MS-DOS-based PCs, and the Apple family of computers.

Lotus, Intel, and Microsoft have announced their support of the digital video interactive (DVI) standard. DVI application development systems are currently being introduced (spring-summer 1988). GE's format adds more than 70 minutes of sound and video to a standard CD-ROM containing text and graphics. The addition of sound and video to a CD-ROM disc is expected to take at least another year of testing and development before it is fully understood.

Challenges to CD-ROM Acceptance

Many industry observers believe that the CD-ROM field is stagnating because of such factors as expensive drives, the lack of applications with sufficient mass appeal, poor user-interface software design, and additional standards affecting such issues as the lack of standardized SCSI ports as well as inadequate product planning to integrate online data with the CD-ROM information system.

Additional factors and new technology developments affecting the future market and product development of CD-ROM technology include the introduction of the interactive compact video disc, CD-I (compact disc-interactive), compact disc write-once (CD-WO), and the latest member of the CD family, the erasable compact disc. CD-WO and write-once, read-many digital optical disk technology on CD-ROM markets will force potential end-users to focus on appropriate application development more strenuously than ever before.

The overwhelming majority of CD-ROM systems and applications are directed toward the IBM and compatibles market. However, during 1987 a growing number of CD-ROM vendors introduced products for the Macintosh and HyperCard. At issue is whether optical disk vendors and manufacturers will offer both IBM and Macintosh versions of a CD-ROM product. When Apple announced its new drive, more than a half dozen Macintosh applications were released (see p. 117). A look at these Macintosh-based products demonstrates Apple's intention to market its HyperCard and new CD-ROM drive as an integrated hardware-software system. These new products include multimedia educational discs, a professional art library for retailer and newspaper advertising departments, and medical software for CD-ROM databases.

Microsoft has introduced several applications with mass appeal such as the Bookshelf and StatPack; it has also funded a prototype CD-ROM called the Multi-Media Encyclopedia which integrates text with images and audio. However, these have yet to make any significant impact on the personal computer market. It is likely that Microsoft's dismantling of its CD-ROM division and the absorption of that division into established product mainstream departments reflects, at best, a retrenchment, and more cautious appraisal of the technology's near future in the mass PC market.

Another concern expressed by many is the relative high cost of CD-ROM drives. The cost of a single drive runs from $800 to $1200. Although several firms such as NEC and Amdek are bundling the drives with applications software, there is, as yet, no apparent trend to use this approach for market development. The latest drive introduced, the AppleSC CD, costs $1,199 and is pricey for the education market that Apple has targeted. As the price of the CD-ROM drive comes down, families may be interested in purchasing electronic versions of encyclopedias such as Grolier Electronic Publishing's 20-volume Academic American Encyclopedia on CD-ROM for $199.

CD-ROM vendors may find it difficult to penetrate the maturing corporate and industrial education and training interactive videodisc markets. It is most likely that CD-ROM will play a significant role as a component in interactive training systems, as it does in the Spectrum Interactive system being developed for American Airlines.

Spectrum Interactive, a company formed by the merger between Interactive Training Systems and Spectrum Training Corporation, and American Airlines have agreed to develop a large-scale, low-cost CD-ROM-based information system for use by agents throughout the SABRE Travel Information Network. SABREVISION will use digital audio encoding, a technology developed by SI that allows for the storage of high-resolution images and audio on CD-ROM. The system will store thousands of full-color images on multiple CD-ROM discs that can be accessed on SABRE's PS/2 workstations and transmitted through LANs (local area networks). We can expect to see a variety of traditional interactive videodisc firms such as Spectrum Interactive integrating CD-ROM technology into existing and new IV training and education systems.

Certainly one of the critical challenges facing the technology is the development of CD-ROM information management software, information retrieval, and storage software that capitalizes on the disc's enormous storage capacity. The focus of software development is on how to fit software to user's needs in face of the enormous storage capacity of a single CD-ROM disc. The development of natural-language query and artificial intelligence are only two of the many approaches that can be expected to encourage users to use the technology.

An example of a new software approach is Knowledge Access International's KAware2 Image System which is designed to store and retrieve large databases that combine both text and images, or images only. This particular software package allows the storage and retrieval of up to 5,000 color images and 50,000 black and white photographs with simultaneous display of text and images. Typical applications include personnel photo files, product catalogs, real estate records, retail merchandising, maps, technical drawings, trademarks, customer signatures, newspaper photo morgues, rare documents, historic preservation archives, museum slides, construction blueprints, inventory and security systems, fingerprints, scientific research data, corporate reports, and mug shots.

The Future of CD-ROM in the Next Decade

Desktop publishing, presentation graphics, and software libraries are likely to be the next growth markets for CD-ROM applications. Optical Media International and Meridian Data are just a few of the growing number of firms offering "premastering" services and workstations for electronic publishing on CD-ROM. Crowninshield Software, Inc. has introduced MediaBase, a database management system designed especially for CD-ROM publishers. A desktop preparation data system, MediaBase allows publishers to combine database management, editing, indexing, and retrieval into a single MS-DOS solution.

NEC Home Electronics is offering Clip Art 3-D, a software title featuring more than 2,500 professionally produced, three-dimensional objects and fonts that can be easily customized by the user for inhouse documents. Another NEC title is Image Folio, which contains more than 4,000 photographic images and an editing program for customizing the TIFF-format files that make up the database. The images range from people to environments to objects.

Today, there are only a few horizontal software packages on the market (examples are Microsoft's Small Business Consultant and Stat-Pack). However, as CD-ROM drives are purchased for integration in professional workstations, software firms such as Borland, Lotus, and others will introduce new software application packages and databases for special-niche markets such as business information.

In some instances we can expect to see CD-ROM replacing microfilm-based systems as in the case of Maxwell Data Management, which will market KnowledgeSet Corporation's CD-ROM information management system to the airline industry for technical documentation use. Another replacement/complement application is Tescor, Inc.'s agreement with Kraus International Publications to market the Kraus Curriculum Development Library on microfiche and CD-ROM. The KCDL includes more than 4,000 K-12 Curriculum Guides in two subject areas reproduced on microfiche. A cumulative index will be placed on the CD-ROM disc that contains Tescor's First National Item Bank.

The special-niche business information market holds great promise for the application and utilization of the technology. A new CD-ROM publication featuring 825,000 real estate transfer records from 1983-1987 for the state of Massachusetts and 1987 for Connecticut is under co-development by Knowledge Access International and Abt Books, Inc. Real estate records are a valuable reference tool for business and consumer marketing information. And, we can expect to see multimedia CD-ROM applications proliferate in the next five years.

Other applications that we can expect to emerge include dissemination of technical documentation and customer support documentation on CD-ROM. The growing interest in storing public-domain software and shareware on CD-ROM signals the emergence of another highly significant market. The Berkeley Mac Users Group (BMUG) will soon publish an anthology on public domain called PD ROM that will sell for less than $100. It has become increasingly apparent to many industry experts that the true market for CD-ROM applications and products is the personal computer market. A cost-benefit application of the technology is the storage and dissemination of computer software and documentation.

Hewlett-Packard (HP) has developed the LaserROM service which is targeted for MIS professionals and managers in systems support and software development. Each significant word on a CD-ROM disc is indexed to provide access to specific information across multiple databases such as HP Communications and Applications Notes. Information can consist of a combination of text, charts, illustrations, and graphics. HP intends to use this monthly subscription service for HP technical and competing customers as well.

There are also some creative and exciting applications of CD-ROM such as a sound effects library for the Macintosh being developed by Farallon Computing and disc manufacturer Discovery Systems (Dublin, OH). This CD-ROM product will combine a broad range of digital recorded sound effects with HyperCard stacks and Farallon's Sound Edit and HyperSound software which will allow the user to search for, screen, select, and manipulate sounds for software development or general entertainment purposes. Sound Edit and HyperSound are gaining rapid acceptance as the standard for digital sound editing, recording , and manipulation in the Macintosh arena.

Summary

In general, the first generation of CD-ROM products has been primarily for storage of large amounts of raw data; many product developers have assumed that simply storing massive amounts of data on a CD would turn it into useful information. In some fields, such as the medi-

The new HP LaserROM service from Hewlett-Packard provides customers with up-to-date support information on HP 3000 Series 900 business computers including the commercial RISC-based HP Precision Architecture computers. Courtesy Hewlett-Packard Company.

cal and library markets, that has been true. However, as users have become more sophisticated and knowledgeable about the technology, they have come to demand that information be *useful,* not simply available in large quantity. The excitement over the technology has been tempered by serious consideration of what the technology can allow. According to Jim Manzi, president of Lotus Development, this technology can free the end-user from spending more time at the computer, online charges, and from information middlemen.

Access to timely, reliable information is a means to achieve competitive advantage. Advances in modern technology have increased our ability to retrieve, analyze, and transform information for a variety of purposes. Information has attained the status of an asset which may be exploited for private advantages. However, the same technologies that have enhanced our ability to access and use information may also limit who will gain access to it. As information professionals, we need to guard against the possibility that CD-ROM technology could contribute to the increasing privatization of information. Touted by many as a development as significant as the printing press, CD-ROM technology should hopefully broaden and expand the depth and breadth of information available to our entire society.

1

Utilization of CD-ROM in the Library

NANCY MELIN NELSON

The largest number of CD-ROM products on the market today are aimed at the library market. The first commercially available CD-ROM product, The Library Corporation's BiblioFile, a cataloging production system, was designed and developed specifically for the library market. Since its introduction in 1985, more than 50 products targeted solely to libraries and information centers have been launched into this vertical market niche.

Librarians* have traditionally been in the business of providing access to information in a variety of forms. Simply stated, they collect books and periodicals, classify their contents, and offer easy access to these materials through catalogs of holdings—either in hard copy, on microform, or as dynamic online systems. Yet for most librarians performing these tasks is only the beginning. Continuing advances in technology now require them to go far beyond these tasks to provide adequate access to library collections.

Massive online database systems, libraries linked by means of mainframe databases, and the growth of computerized services have changed the concept of the traditional library into a "library without walls." Information once thought unavailable may now be identified and requested for local use. In meeting the challenges of enhancing systems through new technologies it has frequently been information brokers, especially those that package data and sell it outside of library walls, that have been in the vanguard of testing and accepting new forms of information retrieval and delivery.

On a daily basis, these information service professionals confront the job of managing an ever-ballooning wealth of data. Images and data are represented by the printed word and other traditional and techno-

*The term "librarian" throughout this chapter is intended to encompass a wide variety of services including those normally associated with information brokers, entrepreneurial professionals, online searchers, and corporate information managers, as well as those traditionally understood as the librarian's.

logical formats, such as videotapes, slides, microforms, realia, manuscripts, online databases, magnetic tapes, software, interactive videodiscs, optical digital disks and, most recently, CD-ROM. Information specialists must not only be aware of sources of data in new media formats, but they must also either acquire them in-house or contract for their use in order to meet the information needs of clients and patrons.

Librarians, as a group, have responded enthusiastically to the introduction of CD-ROM systems despite the new financial and service burdens their use imposes upon them. This chapter assesses the impact of CD-ROM on libraries and information centers and upon the services that entrepreneurs and information brokers provide. It also identifies trends in product development and acceptance, and provides commentary on the significance of the library market niche and a broader non-librarian, consumer acceptance of CD-ROM highly desired by the optical publishing industry.

In order to better appreciate developments in the library market niche, profiles of vendors and their products are used here as examples of successful product development and marketing strategies. These profiles are set against a background that reflects the past 20 years of library automation history as well as the environment of severe budgetary constraints that has affected the adoption of new technologies in libraries and information centers.

Limitations of space dictate that only a representative handful of vendors can be profiled; therefore, exclusion of any particular company does not indicate its lack of success in the market niche. To provide complete reference to all library and information center specialist vendors, a listing of company names and addresses is provided at the end of this chapter.

CD-ROM Market Niche Profile

CD-ROM products developed specifically for the library market can best be classified into two types: (1) those that provide support for processing activities; and (2) those that support access to databases and library/information collections.

This discussion will look separately at three different product applications that currently predominate in this market niche:

- library materials cataloging systems that are basically processing support tools
- online public access catalogs (OPACs)
- CD-ROM versions of reference tools and online databases, both of which offer enhanced and broadened access to local library and other information collections.

Library Processing Profile

The Library Corporation's BiblioFile, a "desk-top catalog production system," is representative of systems offering support for processing activities. BiblioFile contains the complete Library of Congress (LC) MARC (MAchine Readable Cataloging) database of more than 1,500,000 records. This database includes LC holdings both in English and in foreign languages for books, serials, Government Printing Office publications, maps, films, and music scores. These records represent LC acquisitions as far back as 1965.

The database is stored on a minimum of two CD-ROM discs. A basic BiblioFile system configuration includes a single external Hitachi CD-ROM drive while the Enhanced BiblioFile system incorporates as many as four drives making it unnecessary for users to exchange discs as they work with the system. Customers may buy other databases as add-ons. One example is the The Library Corporation's own ANY-BOOK database which includes information about 1,500,000 English-language books in print and is available from 22,000 publishers.

When first introduced at the American Library Association's mid-winter meeting in January 1985, BiblioFile was an instant success. By 1988 the company reported more than 1,000 systems in operation. This phenomenal growth can be attributed primarily to two factors: (1) its extremely low price; and (2) its ability to *replace* costly automated systems dependent on library teleconnections to remote mainframe databases.

Low Prices Produce High Sales. Unlike many other CD-ROM vendors, The Library Corporation (TLC) offers a variety of purchase and subscription packages emphasizing its desire to capture a larger market share through reasonable pricing rather than higher pricing that would result in fewer sales. Its slogan is "pricing puts BiblioFile within easy reach" and the cost to get under way with the system has been described as "positively endearing."

For example, if a library contracts for BiblioFile on a three-year basis, the total price tag is $6,210. Included in this package are the following: monthly CD-ROM updates to the LC MARC English-language cataloging; quarterly disc updates to the company's ANY-BOOK database; a PC-XT-compatible computer with serial and parallel ports; clock/calendar; 640K RAM; a 20-megabyte hard disk; a CD-ROM drive; both MS DOS and BiblioFile software; 800-line support; and hardware replacement via Federal Express for one year.

Company president Brower Murphy has incorporated simplicity of system design and an economical hardware configuration to keep BiblioFile's purchase cost low. To accomplish this objective, develop-

Price List

Pricing puts BiblioFile within easy reach

Catalog Production application software and user manual, and one set of the LC MARC and ANY-BOOK databases on laser disc (annual subscriptions to replacement discs are sold separately — see prices below) . . . .$1750 purchase

International Standard CD-ROM drive with cable that attaches to an IBM-PC or PC-compatible computer . . . .$680 purchase

Application software updates, toll-free 800-line support and hardware maintenance . . . .$540 per year

All the above as complete BiblioFile package . . . .$2930 purchase

Catalog Production Databases

LC MARC ENGLISH LANGUAGE DISCS
Subscription to Library of Congress English-language cataloging data, including monographs, serials, GPO publications, maps, films, and music
Quarterly . . . .$870 per year
Monthly . . . .$1470 per year
LC MARC FOREIGN LANGUAGE DISCS
Subscription to Library of Congress foreign-language cataloging data
Quarterly . . . .$500 per year

Book Identification & Ordering Database

ANY-BOOK DISCS
Quarterly subscription . . . .$600 per year

Additional CD-ROM Equipment and Services

Extra CD-ROM drive, including support for one year . . . .$800 purchase
Conversion of your diskettes to standard OCLC-type MARC tape . . . .$10 per tape
Memory board — upgrade your PC from 256K to a full 640K RAM $185
BiblioFile installation and training . . . .$300 per day
plus expenses

Figure 1. Courtesy The Library Corporation.

ment work on the search software was purposely limited and, as a consequence, it has been described as a "no frills" product. Furthermore, the microcomputer TLC uses in a workstation package is a low-price compatible rather than the top-of-the-line IBM system used by another vendor, the H.W. Wilson Company, for its database systems. As a result, The Library Corporation numbers among its customers many libraries for which installation of the BiblioFile system represents a first automation effort. It may be said with honesty that the advent of CD-ROM in this market niche has, in some cases, actually served to bring librarians into the computer age.

Telecommunications Savings. The second significant attraction inherent in the BiblioFile CD-ROM system is the opportunity to eliminate costly telecommunications connections to remote mainframe computers. Line and connect-time charges have escalated significantly since the divestiture of AT&T. The availability of local access to the complete LC MARC database for unlimited use at no extra charge provides an alternative method of collection maintenance that small libraries simply cannot afford to ignore.

BiblioFile is only one of many CD-ROM-based processing support tools. Several other companies such as OCLC, Inc., EBSCO Electronic Information, and Auto-Graphics, Inc. market similar cataloging systems. It is a tribute to librarians' enthusiastic reception of this new technology that the oldest and largest bibliographic utility, OCLC, Inc., has recognized the potential value of CD-ROM systems. OCLC, originally organized by college librarians in the state of Ohio to offer telecommunications access to the Library of Congress MARC cataloging tapes, is now an international organization.

The Online Computer Library Center (OCLC) was founded in July 1967 to "establish, maintain, and operate a computerized regional library center to serve the academic libraries of Ohio and designed so as to become a part of any national electronic network for bibliographical communication." Over the past 20 years, almost 8,000 libraries in 26 countries in North America and Europe have linked their processing services and other library functions to OCLC headquarters in Dublin, Ohio via dedicated telephone lines or through dial-up access. The company now operates its database of more than 17 million contributed records from nine Xerox Sigma Nine mainframe computers and five smaller ones. These computer systems also provide support for acquiring and cataloging materials as well as for borrowing books and periodicals from other member libraries via an automated interlibrary loan program.

In addition to serving as the de facto "national electronic network," OCLC hàs taken a leadership role in library automation. During the past few years, the company has extended purview of its services into microcomputer program support including the development of its own workstation, national "issues" forums, and support of a variety of initiatives undertaken by major library professional associations.

Yet in spite of its enormous success as measured in numbers of users, the prohibitively expensive costs associated with organizational membership, charges assessed for use of the system, and expenditures for telecommunications links from a library to OCLC have historically precluded many small libraries with budgets ranging in the tens of thousands from linking to OCLC. Indeed, in order to take advantage of OCLC's services, many institutions have established cooperative cataloging centers as a means by which they could spread these costs among several libraries. In these cooperative centers, a small staff, whose salaries and other operating expenses are jointly paid by all members of the cooperative, performs the tasks associated with acquiring, cataloging, and processing books.

OCLC brought automation to the nation's libraries, but it was not always a smooth course it steered. Since it was a new type of organization, many issues arose for which there was no precedent, as has been the case in other automating environments. At first there was a widespread mistrust of "computerized" cataloging. Fears of data loss, frequent downtime as the result of overloaded systems, and concern for losing control over local autonomy were common topics at gatherings of information specialists in the early days of automation.

However, librarians gradually overcame their reluctance to change long held local practices, such as printing subject headings on catalog cards in red, especially as they began to appreciate the direct benefits of automation. These benefits included the a reduction of cataloging backlogs, greater access to local and distant library holdings, and the ease with which computer files, unlike card catalogs, could be searched.

As the benefits began to be realized, information specialists became more demanding about the design and delivery of new and existing systems. The availability of processing support tools such as BiblioFile, with its proven ability to reduce processing costs, has proven to be too attractive to ignore. As OCLC studied the potential for CD-ROM systems in libraries and recognized the enthusiastic reception the new technology was given in this market niche, the company determined to develop and market competing products. Currently it is involved with beta testing its own CD-ROM cataloging product.

Local CD-ROM Cataloging. OCLC's version of a local CD-ROM-based cataloging system will, of course, differ significantly from BiblioFile. Rather than simply produce another CD-ROM containing LC MARC records, OCLC expects to take full advantage of the bibliographic records cooperatively created by its member libraries.

OCLC has announced that it will develop a "family" of CD-ROM discs, each of which will contain approximately 700,000 bibliographic records selected from its database, the Online Union Catalog (OLUC). Each of these records will be linked on the disc to indexes designed specifically for bibliographic records (title, subject, author, etc.). Typical individual discs might contain a database of "records of books most frequently used with imprint dates of 1980 to the present" or "most-used nonbook records plus book records with pre-1980 imprint dates."

Since the Online Union Catalog database is drawn, in part, from a library-created file, the contents for each CD-ROM OCLC markets will not look at all like the BiblioFile database. This new CD-ROM product is certain to appeal to a wide variety of potential users who can expect to find information in the OCLC file that is not in the Library of Congress MARC file. Clearly, like other vendors of CD-ROM "cataloging systems," OCLC has succeeded in identifying and exploiting a feature unique to its system that it can and will use to attract buyers.

Still other vendors, such as EBSCO, for example, emphasize sophisticated software as the special value of their CD-ROM-based cataloging system in order to attract customers. These vendors are principally those that have no unique database and that are able to offer only Library of Congress-produced MARC cataloging records. Many of these vendors, such as Auto-Graphics Inc. and The Library Corporation, for example, have also developed a core client base by successfully shifting existing customers of other print and microform-based cataloging systems to their new product offerings.

While most of these vendors state that specific information regarding numbers of users is proprietary information, regular press releases announcing contract signings provide evidence that these systems are selling well. Libraries have quickly adapted to the use of CD-ROM as a support technology for library cataloging processing activities.

Critical Factors for Marketing Technical Processing Products. Successful strategies for marketing cataloging processing tools, then, include *pricing systems at the low end* to attract customers when they realize the saving potential in CD-ROM systems over links to remote mainframe databases. *Bundling the hardware with the systems* is another appealing feature, particularly for those institutions that can view the system's acquisition on the broader scale of entering the Computer Age. A third factor for success builds on *adding value to the data* such as the development of subject-oriented databases or sophisticated search software. Vendors that have had success in providing cataloging support systems in some other format have been able to convert customer loyalty into CD-ROM system sales.

Online Public Access Catalogs

Steps toward wide-scale automation in libraries, initiated by the dynamic growth of OCLC, created a foundation for the desire to develop local online public access catalogs (OPACs). These OPACs will eventually replace traditional card catalogs or those produced on computer output microform (COM). Computer-based OPACs are desirable because of the ease with which they may be searched by laypeople, the ability to update and thus to provide access to new library holdings quickly, and the significant decrease of labor-intensive and space-demanding aspects of card catalogs. Many libraries have placed outmoded OCLC terminals in public areas as they have upgraded so that library patrons might have the advantage of using them as a substitute for a local computerized catalog. Unfortunately, however, widespread use of the OLUC as a local database never followed.

This failure resulted largely from dissatisfaction and frustration with the use of OCLC's unfriendly search software as well as confusion about what materials were held by the local library. Consequently, many large research libraries began either to purchase minicomputer-based public-access systems from the large community of vendors that now develop and support them, or to fund and design their own.

CD-ROM OPACs in Medium to Small Libraries. Again CD-ROM has proved to be a valuable technology for medium-sized and smaller li-

Figure 2. BiblioFile Intelligent Catalog workstation features spoken help messages. Courtesy The Library Corporation.

braries since it has made it possible to offer automated access to local library holdings. In addition to The Library Corporation, General Research Corporation (GRC) and Brodart Automation have been particularly inventive in the design of an OPAC system.

Like TLC, General Research Corporation has been providing cataloging support systems and services to the library profession for many years. GRC's connection with this market niche extends back for more than two decades. Its CD-ROM-based cataloging system, available for a number of years, is called LaserQuest. In 1987 GRC introduced a sister product, LaserGuide, an online public-access catalog intended to replace COM catalogs.

GRC's LaserGuide incorporates individualized features and as a result has attracted its own particular following in libraries that wish to personalize their systems. The system design includes a map feature that directs a successful searcher to the place in the library where a particular book is stored. LaserGuide also allows the patron to "browse" the bookshelf to learn about other materials that may be of interest, including books on order or in closed collections.

Brodart Automation markets a self-contained Le Pac (for local public

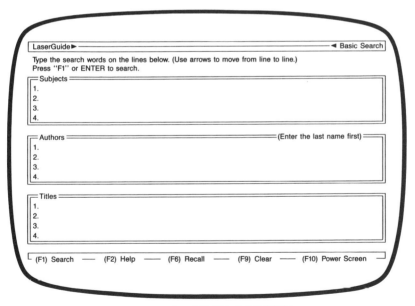

BASIC SEARCH SCREEN

Figure 3. LaserGuide screen. Courtesy General Research Corporation.

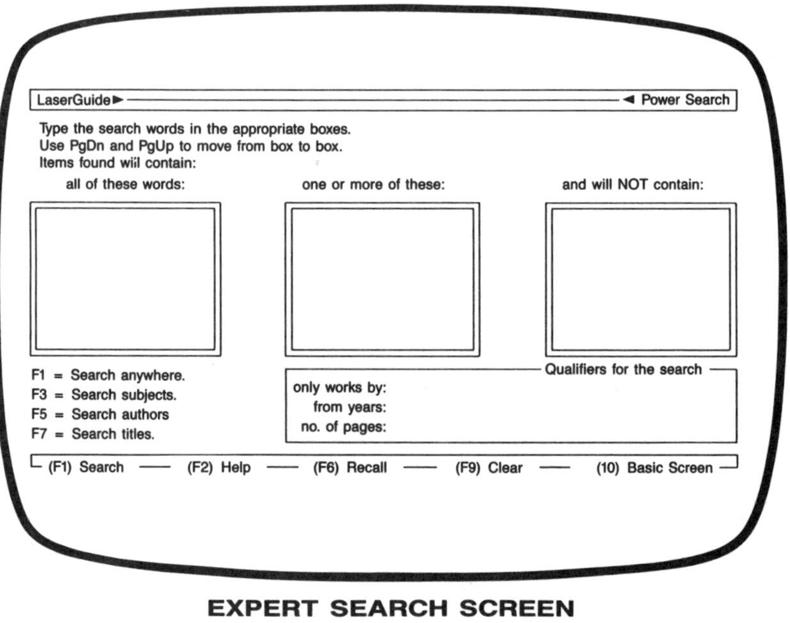

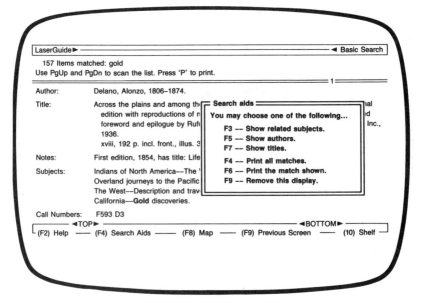

EXPERT SEARCH SCREEN

Figure 4. LaserGuide screen. Courtesy General Research Corporation.

EXPERT AIDS MENU

Figure 5. LaserGuide screen. Courtesy General Research Corporation.

access catalog) system that has gained favor for use as a regional or statewide union catalog. In Pennsylvania, for example, the State Library has coordinated a project to convert 1,400,000 records from 77 public, school, and academic libraries onto the Le Pac CD-ROM system. Brodart has similarly contracted with the states of Kansas and Wisconsin. The perceived benefits to such union catalogs, which may be scoped for searching as local catalogs or for interlibrary loan, include the low costs associated with the shared development of a CD-ROM disc. While individual libraries might not be able to afford the production of CD-ROM discs, regional or statewide projects allow all institutions to mount a local OPAC.

Although initial negative response to CD-ROM OPACs related to delays in updating holdings information, vendors have quickly developed software interfaces that allow librarians to "update" holdings on a resident hard disk as frequently as they desire, even on a daily basis. Turnaround time for completely updated CD-ROM discs is usually offered on a monthly basis. (A write-once optical disk-based OPAC, introduced in 1986 by MARCIVE, Inc., was unsuccessful in this market niche for reasons that will be discussed later in this chapter.)

Critical Factors for the Success of OPACs. Successful strategies in the marketing of online public access catalogs include building in to OPACs some features that will *individualize the local library system. The ability to update CD-ROM systems through a microcomputer hard disk system* is also important to information specialists who, having seen the benefits of such automation in action, find it counterproductive to have local holdings updated on CD-ROM on a monthly or less frequent basis. *Selling systems on a regional or statewide basis* is attractive to librarians who can frequently pay for such systems out of special grants or funding. As with other successful systems, an *affordable price* is a key ingredient for these vendors.

CD-ROM Databases

The success of CD-ROM systems that provide highly visible support for processing services has actually created the market for companies to sell reference databases on CD-ROM. The cost savings associated with the use of CD-ROM databases compared to the costs of those databases to which telecommunications links are required, along with the attendant uncertain pricing structure of online, was not lost on information specialists with limited budgets. The enormous capacity of CD-ROM, making it possible to reduce storage space for hundreds of linear feet of printed indexes or file cabinets full of microfiche databases, was another factor in its quick acceptance by reference specialists. And the ease with which untrained searchers could produce citations was seen as a third advantage of CD-ROM over online or print.

The Library of Congress' MARC database and OCLC's online catalog were only two of many online databases already in digital form and ripe to be converted to CD-ROM format. Librarians, information brokers and entrepreneurs, researchers, and academicians are prime customers for these online databases and use them to support academic and corporate research as well as public information needs at all levels of library service.

Unfortunately, it is almost impossible to estimate the numbers of individual library subscribers to CD-ROM databases. Most companies, wishing to protect proprietary marketing data, will set only a vague sales figure, such as "in the high hundreds." But it is clear from the numbers of workshops, lectures, and references in the professional literature that librarians and patrons are enjoying the benefits of searching extensive databases on CD-ROM rather than online. The primary reason is money.

Libraries, especially those in the public sector that are either municipally or institutionally funded, are traditionally in strong competition for increasingly limited funds. Consequently, they are obliged to allocate their hard-won dollars to serve the greatest number of patrons. CD-ROM systems, offering unlimited searches of databases, fill a role similar to that of printed formats of the same information and guarantee a fixed purchase price that becomes more cost-effective with each search. This is in diametric opposition to the online system cost/use model in which the user must pay again and again even when identical information is retrieved from different databases during a single search session.

As a consequence, librarians have found CD-ROM databases valuable tools particularly for use with students at all levels who are well known to be receptive to changing technologies. Due to limited funds, librarians generally must charge patrons for the costs of online searches and these fees are often prohibitively expensive for students to pay. Thus students characteristically use print-based indexes from which data must be copied by hand. CD-ROM databases, which become more and more cost-effective each time they are searched, allow patrons to walk away from a search with *printed* results.

Librarians have noticed that patrons often misunderstand what the CD-ROM database represents. They have found that too many students believe that what they find from a search of a CD-ROM system represents a search of the whole world of knowledge on a topic. Furthermore, many patrons misunderstand the scope of a CD-ROM database and believe it is a representation of the library's private collection instead of references to a selected dataset, the contents of which may be only partially housed locally. Because CD-ROM searches are generally unmediated, unlike most online searching, librarians are unable to reinforce these distinctions to each individual CD-ROM user.

There is no arguing with success, however. SilverPlatter, Inc. (SP) is now marketing more than 15 different databases on CD-ROM. It has contracted with Information Access Company (IAC) to run SP products on IAC's Reference Center, a system designed to provide multiple workstation access on one network to IAC databases as well as databases provided by other vendors.

SilverPlatter is not unique. Regularly, the firm competes with the H.W. Wilson Company for first place on the "Most Titles on CD-ROM" list. SilverPlatter and H.W. Wilson Company differ significantly, however, and are not competitive with one another for a library's CD-ROM budgets. Until recently, Wilson had only marketed its own proprietary databases on CD-ROM, the same databases it offers in print and online formats. SilverPlatter, on the other hand, has created no databases of its own to market. Instead it has purchased, leased, or otherwise contracted with database owners to market their products on CD-ROMs.

In spring 1988, both companies separately announced a CD-ROM product based on the U.S. Government Printing Office (GPO) Monthly Catalog. Wilson expects to update its product annually and SilverPlatter, bimonthly. Although SilverPlatter has announced a one-time prepublication price of $750, it expects to raise the price to $950, a figure that is in the same range as Wilson's $995. While it will be some time before it is possible to declare a winner on this title, the prospects for high sales of the GPO catalog by each vendor remain solid. Wilson's GPO product will appeal to customers who already subscribe to its other indexes and who are not concerned about the relatively slow updating schedule. SilverPlatter's product, on the other hand, will be demanded in those libraries on college campuses in which goverment documents are valued as research tools and in those depository libraries that house collections of government documents.

Wilson links its CD-ROM product directly to its online system via the Wilsonline Workstation. However, although SilverPlatter will sell equipment to get a library started with its CD-ROM system, the firm has chosen to work with another vendor to provide the online link as well as access to other ondisc/online databases it could not offer before. Users of SilverPlatter will be able to move in a transparent fashion between Information Access Corporation's InfoTrac ondisc/online database, DIALOG's ERIC ondisc/online, and Compact Disclosure's ondisc/online. The ease with which different CD-ROM discs and online systems may be "booted" and searched will appeal to librarians who have had to manipulate hard disk systems to accommodate the differing command files of proprietary systems.

Figure 6. End-user at SilverPlatter workstation. Courtesy SilverPlatter, Inc.

It is clear that successful CD-ROM database vendors are those that aggressively continue to build their product lines. The SilverPlatters and Wilsons have promoted the concept of "families" of CD-ROM discs, a strategy that is being emulated by such other vendors as DIALOG. Once a system user has gained mastery of search software techniques, this skill may be applied across all databases in the firm's family of discs.

Wilson and SilverPlatter have carried the family concept a step further. In SP's case, it markets topically aligned databases such as MED-LINE and ca-CD, Compu-Index and Software CD, and PsycLIT with socioFile. When the Wilson Company completed the task of placing all 14 of its proprietary databases on CD-ROM, it sought and gained rights to market complementary products. Thus it has added the Modern Language Association International Bibliography to complement its Humanities Index, and has included the Index to U.S. Government Periodicals to complement its Index to Legal Periodicals and Social Sciences Index.

As noted before, SilverPlatter has contracted with the Information Access Corporation allowing IAC's InfoTrac Reference Center users to run IAC, SP, and other databases on a single network that incorporates proprietary interface software. Wilson has always offered single workstation access to both WilsonDisc and Wilsonline products, a feature it has made particularly attractive through a special no-cost post-CD-ROM search dial-up feature. It seems likely that other vendors will follow the IAC strategy to increase the use of their own CD-ROM databases. If they do, CD-ROM systems ought to become even more popular as reference and research tools. If librarians, information brokers, and others are able to move across systems with greater ease, one perceived impediment to their use—the need to reboot proprietary systems—will be reduced if not eliminated.

Pricing, Ease of Use, Hardware

Vendors such as The Library Corporation, H.W. Wilson, and SilverPlatter that are thriving in this market niche are able to attribute their success to attractive pricing options, aggressive production of complementary CD-ROM systems, and systems that are easy to acquire and use. By and large, when they are queried about these systems, librarians identify four problem areas:

- high-priced systems
- one system/one user restrictions
- lack of market stability
- lack of product innovation

Successful vendors in this marketplace have, to a large extent, kept their prices low (BiblioFile) or offered options that have made it possible for librarians to incrementally add new databases and hardware (H.W. Wilson and SilverPlatter) as funding has become available. SP does not market a workstation but will sell drives, interfaces, and cabling at very low prices, a feature that is designed to encourage subscription to its systems. Few vendors are eager to get into the business of maintaining hardware, and most companies that sell proprietary workstations offer restricted warranties and charge for service contracts.

Successful companies are also in a constant cycle of adding new products. As noted earlier, H.W. Wilson and SilverPlatter regularly trade places as the vendor with the greatest number of CD-ROM products. New product announcements serve to assure their customers that these companies are in the CD-ROM business to stay. In a similar vein, The Library Corporation now markets its products as three separate systems--the Catalog Production station, the Catalog Maintenance station, and its latest, the Intelligent Catalog, a multimedia public-access catalog. This tactic calls attention to the different functions TLC systems provide, establishes their usefulness in different parts of the library, and persuades the customer to purchase "compatible" CD-ROM equipment and products.

Ease-of-use is another hallmark of systems developed by successful vendors. According to reports and reviews published in such journals as *CD-ROM Librarian, Wilson Library Bulletin, Optical Information Systems, Small Computers in Libraries, Online, CD-ROM Review,* and other professional sources, information users have adapted quickly to requirements for effectively searching these systems. While SP products may on occasion be compared unfavorably with other CD-ROM databases produced by competing organizations due primarily to their lack of complexity, the bottom line is that SP's products are selling. The competitive pricing structure developed by SP combined with the great numbers of systems it offers, and the topical linkage of these systems, account for the company's success.

Technology Cycle

Because libraries and information centers serve principally as the repositories of information for books, periodicals, online databases, video and audio, analog recordings, and magnetic software among other formats, issues of preservation, access, storage, and security run as themes throughout library literature and at professional gatherings of information specialists. CD-ROM systems address and at least partially resolve many of these issues.

It is likely that we can expect CD-ROM products to become as commonplace as microform systems within a few years. Most vendors report that delays in purchase are simply attributable to funding difficulties to which librarians have responded with imagination.

Other types of optical technology appear at this time to have a limited market penetration. Interactive videodiscs, for example, might become a part of those library collections that serve large populations

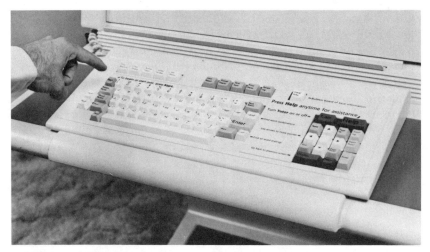

Figure 7. BiblioFile Intelligent Catalog's specially designed, user-friendly keyboard. Courtesy The Library Corporation.

in the education niche. CD-I (compact disc-interactive) is expected to appeal to the entertainment consumer market and is likely to fill the same role as compact audiodiscs and videotapes in libraries (i.e., consumer items that libraries purchase, stock, and circulate to patrons).

It may be that systems based in write-once, read-many (WORM) optical disk technology have a small potential market in libraries. As noted earlier, a WORM-based online public-access catalog was introduced by the MARCIVE Corporation of San Antonio, Texas, two years ago; its appearance was brief. The company is convinced that its failure can be attributed to the fact that librarians were simply not prepared to accept a second, different hardware issue at a time when they were adjusting to CD-ROM technology.

Hybrid Systems

Hybrid systems that combine either CD-ROM and magnetic hard disks or CD-ROM with direct modem links to remote mainframe computers have been received favorably. The first type of hybrid system is now being used widely in cataloging and online public-access catalog systems. The second type of system is being used with CD-ROM versions of popular online databases. The popularity of hybrid systems may be explained by the ease of updating local databases and conducting reference searches. Equipment is self-contained and requires little additional capital outlay for libraries that may already own the requisite hardware.

The Future

Librarians who have become especially interested in CD-ROM product development complain that insufficient attention is being paid to determining what products are well suited for integration into library collections. Instead, they believe that CD-ROM system vendors are making development decisions with insufficient concern for or understanding of how libraries operate and what libraries need for their patrons.

Librarians are convinced that they have two roles to play in the growth of this industry. First, as users of the technology they are serving as unofficial consultants to vendors regarding the efficacy of the CD-ROM, specific uses for the technology, concerns related to hardware and security issues, and the development of new and enhanced systems.

More significant, however, librarians see their broader role all too frequently overlooked by vendors that can only understand this market niche as a narrow one. That role is to serve as unpaid demonstrators and promoters of CD-ROM to the larger consumer market. These systems are expensive, frequently beyond the budgets of individuals or small companies. Their availability in libraries makes it possible for people to use and become familiar with them toward the day when they will be priced low enough to be affordable.

It is well known that many "business" products are being marketed solely to offices. Microsoft's Bookshelf is one example. What vendors do not understand, however, is that a large portion of the business community relies solely on local public libraries and specialized public library reference collections and services to support its ongoing business. These are the hundreds of thousands of persons that Microsoft is trying to reach. By ignoring the potential of these absolutely free and unsolicited product and system demonstrations, many firms are acting in a shortsighted manner. Undoubtedly, thousands of dollars will be spent on advertising, dollars that could be put to better use by using the direct services of library consultants in product and market niche development.

Librarians as Innovators

As they have embraced the benefits of CD-ROM technology and devised ways to cope with the new problems and issues it brings into the library, librarians have proved to be an excellent test environment for the industry. What information service professionals now must do is to aggressively identify and prioritize those databases that should ideally be converted to or created on CD-ROM. Furthermore, they must provide data to underscore to vendors the market significance of these applications.

Company Index

Auto-Graphics, Inc.
3201 Temple Avenue
Pomona, CA 91768
800-325-7961
800-828-9585 (CA)

R. R. Bowker Company
Electronic Publishing
245 West 17th Street
New York, NY 10011
212-645-9700

The British Library
Research and Development Department
2 Sheraton Street
London W1V 4BH, England
01-636-1544

Brodart Co.
Library Automation Division
500 Arch Street
Williamsport, PA 17705
800-233-8467
and
10983 Via Frontera
San Diego, CA 92127
800-643-0523

Cataloging Distribution Service (CDS)
Customer Services Section
The Library of Congress
Washington, DC 20541
202-287-1678

DIALOG Information Services, Inc.
3460 Hillview Avenue
Palo Alto, CA 94304
800-3-DIALOG
415-858-3785

EBSCO Electronic Information Division
EBSCO Subscription Services
P.O. Box 13787
Torrance, CA 90503
213-530-7533

The Faxon Company
15 Southwest Park
Westwood, MA 02090
617-329-3350

General Research Corporation
5383 Hollister Avenue
P.O. Box 6770
Santa Barbara, CA 93160-6770
800-235-6788
805-964-7724

Information Access Company
11 Davis Drive
Belmont, CA 94002
800-227-8431
415-591-2333

Information Technology Publishing
ALA Publishing Services
American Library Association
50 East Huron Street
Chicago, IL 60611
312-944-6780

JA Micropublishing, Inc.
271 Main Street
Box 218
Eastchester, NY 10107
914-793-2130

The Library Corporation
P.O. Box 40035
Washington, DC 20016
800-624-0559

Library Systems & Services, Inc.
A Gaylord Bros. Company
1395 Piccard Drive, Suite 100
General Motors Building
Rockville, MD 20850
301-258-0200

MARCIVE, Inc.
P.O. Box 47508
San Antonio, TX 78265
800-531-7678

National Information Center for Educational Media (NICEM)
Access Innovations, Inc.
P.O. Box 40130
Albuquerque, NM 87196
800-421-8711
505-265-3591

OCLC, Inc.
6565 Frantz Road
Dublin, OH 43017-0702
800-848-5878
614-764-6000

PAIS Compact Disc Database
Public Affairs Information Service
11 West 40th Street
New York, NY 10018-2693
212-736-6629

Research Publications
900 Armour Drive
Lake Bluff, IL 60044
312-234-1220

SilverPlatter Information Services, Inc.
37 Walnut Street
Wellesley Hills, MA 02181
617-239-0306
800-343-0064

University Microfilms International
300 North Zeeb Road
Ann Arbor, MI 48106
313-761-4700

Utlas International
8300 College Boulevard
Overland Park, KS 66210
800-338-8537
913-451-3111

Western Library Network
Washington State Library
Mail Stop AJ-11W
Olympia, WA 98504-0111
206-459-6518

H.W. Wilson Company
950 University Avenue
Bronx, NY 10452
212-588-8400

2
Using CD-ROM in Science and Medicine

PATTI MYERS

S cientific and health care professionals have always had extensive informational needs. Not only do they need the most current data (i.e., latest breakthroughs), they also require completeness—all the available information—in order to perform their work. In addition to standardized languages and abbreviations, extensive print resources, and highly focused sources such as specialized libraries, information centers, and associations, these professionals have adopted electronic information-gathering techniques such as online searching and electronic transfer of data (via online or magnetic tapes) into their own computer centers. So essential is current and accurate information to science and medical professionals that these fields have been leaders in information techniques and technological applications.

This chapter will highlight how CD-ROM discs are being used in these fields. The majority of CD-ROM products available today are alternatives to existing information products/services. In some cases, the CD-ROM disc actually replaces another information distribution technology. In other cases the CD-ROM disc complements existing technologies. Whether these CD-ROM discs serve to replace or supplement existing resources depends largely on two factors: the applications software and the scope of the data contained on the CD-ROM. Only recently have emerging CD-ROM products suggested how CD-ROM technology may more dramatically enhance and broaden the scope of scientific and medical information access.

Primary Uses and Applications

Today there are four primary uses of CD-ROM-based products:

- obtaining data to apply to research
- obtaining data for publishing
- bibliographic searching
- ongoing reference

Bibliographic and reference titles represent the lion's share of current CD-ROM products.

Electronic Data for Scientific Research

Many scientific agencies and institutions gather data directly through computers (such as satellite-gathered readings and images captured and transmitted from space) or input reported data into their computer systems. Data may then be used for such purposes as research analysis and comparative evaluations with previously captured data. While reports may highlight such scientific data in published findings, reports, etc., many scientists may want access to the data for their own studies on similar or related topics. Mass volumes of data are often analyzed again, usually on a scientist's own computer system. In order to avoid re-entering data into local computer systems, an electronic version of the data is preferred for ongoing scientific research.

There have been two primary methods for obtaining large volumes of information in its electronic form:

- online transfer of data (via a direct telecommunications link or an online service)
- transfer of data onto magnetic tapes and shipment of tapes to the person requesting the data

Either of these options can accommodate special requests to "package" data or only selected portions of the data into a form that would be readily useful to the data seeker. The availability of specially prepared data depends on the information provider's willingness to prepare a custom version. More often, a standard "package" of fielded data is prepared for distribution. The researcher may then need to do extra programming or editing in order to have the data in forms suitable for individual projects.

Even with a higher-speed communications link, the online transfer of large volumes of scientific data can be expensive, with long transmission times. The online option is more practical for small amounts of selected data or for quick receipt of the very latest data.

The second option, magnetic tapes and/or disks, requires more time for the information provider to transfer (write) data onto reels of tape (or disks), verify accuracy, prepare the tape/disk for shipping, and includes the information user's waiting time while information is written and transported. Once received, the information user must exercise care in handling and storing the magnetic media that require controlled environments, floor space for archiving, and large pieces of hardware.

CD-ROM technology is a welcomed third option in scientific research and monitoring endeavors. CD-ROM discs can hold huge volumes of scientific data (equal to the data stored on 10 1600 bits per inch [bpi] magnetic tapes), yet do not require the special handling, storage space, or large drives necessary for magnetic media. Shipping costs are greatly reduced as well. In addition, the mass production process for CD-ROM discs (versus one-at-a-time writing of magnetic media) can mean less time for creating multiple copies of the database.

There are, however, some drawbacks to this distribution technique. Unless a significant number of science professionals are interested in the data, mass reproduction of the data may not be warranted. The mass production process also means no "custom versioning" of the database by the information provider and less immediate access than online techniques offer.

To illustrate CD-ROM-based distribution of data for subsequent, computer-based research, let us take a look at a few representative titles. Hydrodata is designed for water-resource professionals to analyze water needs in the western United States. In addition to software for evaluating data, the publishers (U.S.WEST, Knowledge Engineering, and WBLA, Inc.) distribute the U.S. Geological Service Daily Values for the western states—including more than 100 years of river flow, quality, and lake measurements—on CD-ROM.

The Department of Atmospheric Sciences at the University of Washington has published the Gale Experiment Set on CD-ROM. This CD-ROM database contains surface upper air meteorological data during Genesis of Atlantic Lows. Its National Meteorological Grid Point Data Set CD-ROM contains meteorological information about the northern hemisphere from the 1940s to the 1980s.

NASA is sponsoring the development of a CD-ROM product that will contain two collections of planetary science data from the University of Colorado's Laboratory for Atmospheric and Space Physics (LASP). The resulting CD-ROM disc will be distributed to scientific research organizations and planetary scientists. The University of Colorado LASP is already distributing, on a controlled release basis, images of Uranus, its satellites, and its rings with its Voyager II Images of Uranus.

When the purpose of the CD-ROM product is to foster subsequent computer analysis, a primary consideration is compatibility of the data with selected computers and analysis programs. In cases such as the Hydrodata CD-ROM, software is provided by the publisher, assuring certain capabilities. In other cases, the publisher has to conform to existing standards or to the majority of already-installed research tools (e.g., field identifiers, operating systems, analysis software, hardware) in order to provide compatibility in a range of situations.

Software is another type of data that is needed in electronic form.

Rather than re-entering source codes or obtaining individual programs on floppy diskettes, a CD-ROM disc can provide numerous programs and timely updates. PC-SIG is a disc containing the equivalent of 705 floppy diskette-based software programs. In addition to general-purpose programs such as spreadsheet, statistical programs, genealogy programs, etc., and various programming languages, the CD contains a variety of programs specifically developed for science and biomedical uses. For example, one program provides files for use in Nuclear Magnetic Resonance Spectroscopy; another program for hospital pharmicists helps in the mixing of intravenous solutions.

Electronic Data for Publishing

Publishing is an integral part of the scientific and health care fields, since relevant scientific knowledge and research must be shared and accessible for further study, peer review, and ongoing reference.

In scientific, medical, and health care fields, publishing (or republishing) is another activity that, increasingly, requires data to be in electronic (versus print) form. In addition to needing direct access to data for research, information, etc., the user may also need to incorporate that data (along with new data) into a final report. The final report may be in hard copy (paper) or electronic.

To reuse the data for publishing ultimately requires importing data into a word processing and/or composition program, creating a final manuscript. Textual data, once in electronic form, usually does not have to be re-keyed in the creation of the final manuscript (although the user must have some technique for transferring the data into an acceptable form and into the proper location in the manuscript). The source of the text (CD-ROM, magnetic media, or communications-based) does not significantly alter the transfer process. It is possible, however, to package software with the data to streamline the transfer and publishing formatting processes. Medical libraries, for example, have been able to easily generate catalog cards and listings from electronic bibliographic files.

In most cases, the primary focus of the CD-ROM product is in the distribution of data; what may happen later (such as publishing a report containing data obtained from a CD-ROM) is of little or no significance. A primary exception involves graphics.

Graphics require special consideration because compatibility issues are involved. One of the more experienced producers of graphic data on optical disks, Geovision, Inc., has developed a system to complement its CD-ROM library of maps and other graphic and geographic materials. The system has a proprietary applications program called "On the World," running under Microsoft's "Windows." With Windows, graphic data from the CD-ROM disc can be used with selected word processing programs and graphics application programs such as Media Cybernetics's Halo and Autodesk, Inc.'s Autocad. Unless provisions for data exchange among programs is provided, scientific and medical professionals must resort to more manual means (e.g., conventional photography, new artwork, image scanning) for publishing graphics.

Locating Information and Sources—Bibliographic Databases

Printed bibliographies have been essential in both scientific and medical endeavors. In health care, for example, appropriate patient diagnosis and care requires not only accurate and up-to-date information, but also assessment of the entire range of information that may be relevant and applicable. Since no individual health care professional could possibly read all the new medical articles, reports, findings, books, etc., published each month, bibliographies are an important method for locating newly published information.

Various biomedical bibliographic publications have been developed over the years. These print bibliographies differed primarily in scope (e.g., which source publications are indexed, topics indexed), frequency of publication, and extent of bibliographic citation (e.g., citations only, citations with abstracts, citations with peer reviews of selected articles). With thousands of new biomedical articles published each month, large volumes of bibliographies became necessary. In order to keep current, frequent printed supplements or editions were also needed.

In medical libraries, microfilm versions became an attractive, space-saving alternative. Even more advantageous were online bibliographic databases—where updates were quickly available, a wide range of years could be searched at one time, and the contents of multiple bibliographies could be searched simultaneously. MEDLINE, for example, provides access to a wide range of biomedical literature from 3,600 journals, corresponding in part to the coverage in Index Medicus, Index to Dental Literature, and International Nursing Index, with citations from 1964 to the previous month. Especially important to evolving biomedical online bibliographic efforts has been the development of standard Medical Subject Headings (called MeSH) by the National Library of Medicine. The MeSH nomenclature is used for citation keywords and headings, providing more precise searching of bibliographic records.

Most current scientific and health care CD-ROM discs are versions of online bibliographies. A major potential benefit of a CD-ROM version over the online equivalent is the fixed cost compared to the variable costs associated with online searching. Whether this can be considered a benefit depends on the amount of online use charges compared with the annual cost of the disc. There are now eight CD-ROM versions of MEDLINE (these will be discussed in more detail later), plus numerous other bibliographic discs, usually targeted to specific disciplines, some of which are discussed here.

AGRICOLA (one version is available from SilverPlatter, Inc. for $1,750 per year with quarterly updates covering 1983 to present, and another version is available from OCLC) provides a bibliography of agricultural data.

socioFile contains bibliographic citations and in-depth abstracts of articles from 1,500 serials and citations of relevant dissertations, covering sociology literature from 1974 to the present. This CD-ROM subscription is a cooperative effort between Sociological Abstracts Database Services and SilverPlatter, Inc. ($1,950 per year with updates).

PsycLIT consists of psychology and behavioral science citations, also available from SilverPlatter, Inc. ($3,995 per year with updates).

Ccinfodisc contains the Canadian Centre for Occupational Health & Safety online databases. Series A is chemical data and Series B is OHS information ($100 [Canadian]/year with updates).

The following CD-ROM discs are more generalized bibliographic discs in the science and health care fields:

- H.W. Wilson's Applied Science & Technology Index ($1,495 per year).
- H.W. Wilson's General Science Index ($1,295 per year).
- H.W. Wilson's Social Science Index ($1,295 per year— with each annual subscription of a Wilson CD-ROM comes unlimited access to the Wilsonline [online] version of the corresponding database).
- Science Citation Index from the Institute for Scientific Information contains indexes of print products and additional access points for 1986, 1987, or 1988 materials ($1,500 to $10,200 per year for a single subscription).
- NTIS CD-ROM from OCLC provides the National Technology Information Service index and abstracts of published reports of government-sponsored research.
- NTIS CD-ROM discs from SilverPlatter come in two forms: (1) the five-year set, which includes the last five years of complete bibliographic citations to government-sponsored research and development reports; and (2) discs containing one of four subsets of the entire NTIS database for selected disciplines, as follows:

  1) NTIS: Environmental Health and Safety
  2) NTIS: Computers, Communications and Electronics

3) NTIS: Medicine, Health Care and Biology
4) NTIS: Aeronautics, Aerospace & Astronomy

Another potential benefit of a CD-ROM version is the possibility of simultaneously searching multiple bibliographies. Such simultaneous searching of different databases is possible on the OSH-ROM from SilverPlatter, Inc. ($900 a year with semi-annual updates). OSH-ROM combines several databases from different vendors on the same disc: NIOSHTIC from the National Institute for Occupational Safety and Health; HSELINE from the Health and Safety Executive Library and Information Services in the United Kingdom; and CISDOC from the Labour Office of International Occupational Safety and Health Information Centre in Geneva. Similarly, Cambridge Scientific Abstracts, a provider of scientific data through six online databases and 30 scientific journals, has repackaged its bibliographic databases in some CD-ROM products.

One is ASFA Aquatic Science and Fisheries which contains 110,000 abstracts of international research in aquatic biology, fisheries, limnology, oceanography, earth sciences, marine technology, living and non-living resources, and related issues ($2,250 per year). Another Cambridge disc is entitled Life Sciences and contains abstracts of articles published after January 1983 on biological, medical, and ecological topics ($3,150 per year).

Another interesting example of combining databases is the result of a cooperative effort among EMBASE (an online database provider), SilverPlatter, Inc. (a CD-ROM developer), the Yearbook Medical Press, and the National Library of Medicine (NLM). The disc, ca-CD (Cancer Abstracts), combines EMBASE cancer-related bibliographies from 1984 to the present, with the last two years of CANCERLIT citations and the last three years of "Yearbook of Cancer," without any duplicate citations. The ca-CD record will combine any unique fields of the three different files (e.g., EMBASE fields for trade and manufacturer names, MALINET descriptors, CANCERLIT's special fields) and the in-depth Yearbook of Cancer abstract and physician comments. Elsevier will publish discs quarterly and charge an annual subscription rate of $2,500.

Referencing Data

Reference CD-ROM discs are largely made up of the actual information a scientist or health care professional needs. Access may be through bibliographic-type delimiters and searching techniques. However, the disc supplies full-text articles and/or fielded data for immediate reference. The CD-ROM disc may either replace or supplement printed reference books and online full-text databases. Typically, reference CD-ROM discs are focused on very specific topics, providing compact, complete reference materials that can be readily queried at a fixed cost (versus variable online costs depending on time of use).

Reference CD-ROM discs may contain large amounts of numerical, fielded data. One example of a fielded, non-bibliographic reference CD-ROM disc is Chem-bank, from SilverPlatter, Inc. This disc contains three separate databases of information on hazardous chemical substances, designed for use by qualified subject-matter experts (as opposed to the general public or causal researcher). The Registry of Toxic Effects of Chemical Substances (RTECS) database provides detailed information on the toxic effects of more than 85,000 chemical substances on living, animal tissue. Each substance record may contain up to 19 fields of data. Another database, Oil and Hazardous Materials—Technical Assistance Data System (OHM-TADS) produced by the Environmental Protection Agency, describes in length (with up to 120 fields per record) the properties, hazards, environmental implications, handling, and disposal features of 1,400 commodity chemicals.

Chemical Hazard Response Information System (CHRIS) is produced by the U.S. Coast Guard to describe 1,000 or so chemicals and appropriate methods of handling emergencies, such as spills involving these chemicals. Most records contain between 70 and 99 fields of data about each chemical. Portions of Chem-bank may be used by a variety of professionals in toxicology, industrial hygiene, public health, environmental protection, government regulatory groups, and companies involved in disposal or transport of hazardous materials.

Other fielded reference CD-ROM discs include International Center for Diffraction Data's Powder Diffraction File on chemical compounds, Occupation Health Services' OHS MSDS on Disc containing Material Safety Data Sheets, and John Wiley & Sons' Registry of Mass Spectral Data which also contains special software programs. Some of these discs, such as CD/Biotech, may also be useful for scientists who wish to apply selected data (without re-keying) to experimental models, etc.

Full-Text Reference CD-ROM Discs

Full-text CD-ROM discs are another type of reference disc. Some of these are encyclopedic in nature, providing the user with a compact alternative or supplement to large printed volumes. John Wiley & Sons offers two such products: Kirk-Othermer Encyclopedia of Chemical Technology (a reference work on chemistry and the chemical industry, with about 1,200 articles that in print comprises 24 volumes), and the

Mark Encyclopedia of Polymer Science & Engineering (ultimately containing 19 volumes of polymer and plastics reference work plus additional engineering and processing coverage).

Another CD-ROM reference work is the dictionary. Wiley is publishing a CD-ROM version of The International Dictionary of Medicine & Biology. The disc will contain the entire dictionary—including graphic illustrations and definitions of more than 160,000 biomedical terms—which currently occupies three printed volumes.

McGraw-Hill is combining one of its popular dictionaries with an encyclopedia. The McGraw-Hill CD-ROM Science & Technical Reference Set contains 7,300 encyclopedia articles and 98,500 terms with 115,000 definitions. The primary benefits of the McGraw CD-ROM reference is improved information referencing rather than space savings. This system provides for window overlays to view definitions while reviewing an article, highlighting search terms within articles to quickly pinpoint desired information, and several searching techniques.

The earliest medical reference CD-ROM product was the Computerized Clinical Information System (CCIS) from Micromedex Inc. CCIS consists of four different databases: Drugdex (drug evaluations); Emerindex (critical care abstracts); Identidex (tablet and capsule identifications); and Posindex (toxicology database). Since 1974 Micromedex had been distributing these references on microfiche to hospitals for hospital-based physicians, nurses, and pharmacists; magnetic tape versions are also distributed. With the advent of growing numbers of personal computers in health care environments, consideration was given to online distribution, but CD-ROM was chosen as a preferable means (due largely to the potential to develop searching techniques that could be easily and directly used by the health professional).

Just emerging now are new types of CD-ROM reference products, which may be considered anthologies of a sort. One type of CD-ROM anthology compiles, on a frequent basis, the full-text of selected articles from a variety of journals. The ADONIS CD-ROM Biomedical Collection is such a product, with 50,000 full-text articles from more than 200 biomedical journals published by Pergamon, Blackwell, Elsevier, Springer-Verlag, Butterworth, Churchill Livingston, Mosby, Munjsgaard, Thieme, and John Wiley & Sons. The disc is updated weekly, providing health professionals with a compact means to easily and instantly access the full-text of current biomedical articles. Another set of CD-ROM anthologies is produced by Ellis Enterprises: The Physician Library and The Nurse Library. Each health care anthology is a compilation of textbooks, manuals for major specialties, and in the Nursing Edition board examination aids, forms, and nursing plans. The physician version sells for $995; the nurse version for $795.

Another type of emerging CD-ROM reference is the comprehensive full-text anthology of information on a specific topic. Rather than covering a broad spectrum of scientific or medical data, these products focus on a single topical area, providing a deeper, richer reference collection on the subject. One such CD-ROM, the Data Archive on Adolescent Pregnancy & Pregnancy Prevention from Sociometrics Corp. and Knowledge Access, Inc., consists of more than 100 major studies of teenage sexual behavior including more than 40,000 variables. Another example of this new genre CD-ROM is called COMPACT LIBRARY: AIDS from the Medical Publishing Group. This disc, which will be updated quarterly, contains more than 2,000 full-text articles plus about 11,000 MEDLINE citations related to AIDS. Such full-text references are sometimes referred to as "knowledge bases" or "electronic textbooks," providing the user with a compact, in-depth, desktop database.

Issues Affecting CD-ROM Use in Scientific and Health Care Applications

To date the applications for CD-ROM in science, medicine, and health care have focused on replacing or supplementing other methods of information distribution and access. The benefits of CD-ROM technology over existing distribution and access forms (namely, print, microforms, magnetic tape, and online) vary. While information providers may focus on the benefits of one distribution means over another, the information user is also concerned with the applicability of a CD-ROM in terms of subject relevancy and perceived changes to current methods of information access and use.

For scientists and health care professionals who frequently use computer workstations in their work, the focus is fourfold:

1) The need for and applicability of the data: how frequently is data needed? How comprehensive must the data be? How current? How will the data be used?

2) The trade-offs among other distribution methods: ease-of-use; ease and speed of accessing desired data; space requirements; data availability; one-time costs and ongoing costs; value-added characteristics, etc.

3) The hardware requirements for use: what additional drives, ports, memory, input/output devices, etc., are necessary? Does the work environment accommodate the necessary hardware? Does the required hardware complement current operations and techniques? Are hardware requirements applicable to other CD-ROM products?

4) The software aspects of the product: is the operating system compatible? Does searching require learning new skills? How difficult

is locating data? Does the software complement current searching/ accessing skills? How difficult is using data? Is the software "bugfree" or "evolving"? Is the software well-documented and supported?

For those science and health care professionals such as researchers and medical librarians who rely for much of their information needs on intermediaries and who are not themselves frequent computer users, the primary issues differ. Of utmost importance is the ease with which they can locate all the desired information, plus the time and the costs associated with obtaining the data. At least initially, there is less concern about such issues as compatibility and standards.

Experienced and Novice Searchers

To date the majority of CD-ROM products have been targeted to professional researchers and information intermediaries. In health care, for example, target markets for CD-ROM products are typically medical libraries and health care institutions where professional information specialists assist physicians, administrators, hospital staff, and students in information searches. Professional information specialists tend to view CD-ROM products not as substitutes for other media, but as viable products for subsets of information needs.

As information seekers gain familiarity with personal computers and the potential richness of electronic access, there is growing interest (from both users and intermediaries) in the user directly accessing and using data. In order to "attract" direct users, CD-ROM product developers must offer sufficient improvements over existing (usually printed) access methods. There are three major issues for attracting science and health care users.

- the information content of the disc (subject matter and scope in terms of years, currency, quality of data, completeness of data, and type of data—text, graphics, sound, etc.)
- amount of training required for use
- range of features for accessing the data

The latter items (training and features) relate to the applications software of the product.

Applications Software Is the Key

The applications software of a CD-ROM product is critical, both at the level of a professional researcher/information specialist and that of the more casual information seeker. Even though the desire for natural query languages may be less of an issue in science and medicine (due to the technical, specific nature of scientific and medical terminology), users want the means to easily locate all pertinent data in a timely, efficient manner.

In addition to natural query languages are a variety of specific searching features to help locate data, including the following:

- the extent to which data can be searched (e.g., selected fields only, all fields, any word, any phrase)
- proximity options
- "wild card" options
- browsing capabilities
- highlighted keywords and phrases within text
- the ability to look up a definition, reference, etc., while viewing an article (i.e., hypertext functions)
- menus or prompts to guide the user through creating search requests
- the option to bypass menus/prompts (for more skilled searchers)
- the ability to find related terms
- functions to locate proper terminology and spelling
- single key access to a record directly from a listing
- the ability to save, compile, and apply previous search criteria
- easy "swapping" of discs to search other databases without resetting search parameters
- access to "Help" features at any point during the searching process

Many science and medical CD-ROM discs offer simple, easy-to-use menus as well as a command language for the more expert searchers. While menus help the more inexperienced user create Boolean search parameters, use of precise terminology remains important. For example, when searching medical bibliographies, use of the MeSH terms usually yields a more complete and precise listing than searches that do not include MeSH terms.

More recent (1987-1988) medical and science CD-ROM products have more features to allow sophisticated searching, even by novices. For example, the CD-ROM edition of Science Citation Index from the Institute for Scientific Information has enhanced indexes (compared to its print version), browsing, and a feature called "related records" that allows the user, with a single keystroke, to request the system to locate all other items in the 600,000-item database that have the same author references as the item being viewed.

Even after data is located, applications software continues to play a role. How much of the item is viewable on the screen at one time? Does it allow the user to page up and down within a listing or does it restrict motion? Does the system handle graphics? How does the user generate hardcopy or store copy onto magnetic media? When generating a printout must the user wait until printing is complete? Again, the newer products show advances. For instance, the McGraw-Hill Encyclopedia and Directory shows a full screen of text, allows scrolling in both directions, and provides for quick transfer of an entire article to magnetic disk or printer. Other products lack some of these features.

To date, there has been limited graphics handling software for medical and scientific CD-ROM discs. Except for those discs made up primarily of images (the Geovision maps and NASA images of Uranus), only one science/medical CD-ROM disc (the McGraw reference set) deals with images. To access the stored graphics images (monochrome illustrations and photographs) requires special additional components (Reference Technology's image-processor, a host adapter card, and a high-resolution monitor) which cost considerably more than the $300 CD-ROM disc and the $1,000 drive.

Eight MEDLINE CD-ROM Discs and How They Differ

To illustrate the range and nature of differences among medical CD-ROM discs, this section will consider some of the variations among eight products, all of which are CD-ROM versions of MEDLINE. As described earlier, MEDLINE is a bibliographic database with citations from more than 3,000 biomedical journals, compiled by the National Library

Figure 8. SilverPlatter's MEDLINE CD-ROM disc. Courtesy SilverPlatter, Inc.

of Medicine. MEDLINE is available through at least 10 online services. Presently, eight companies also offer a CD-ROM MEDLINE product.

Hardware Variations

All but one of the CD-ROM discs are used on IBM-PCs or compatibles, although memory requirements vary from 256K to 640K. This hardware choice is not surprising since the IBM-PC is increasingly used in medical libraries and professional information intermediaries for online searching. The single exception is Aries Systems Corporation's Knowledge Finder, which runs on a Macintosh Plus, SE or Mac II, and is targeted for direct use by the information seeker.

MEDLINE on SilverPlatter and BRS's Colleague Disc can be used on a Sony, Hitachi, or Philips CD-ROM drive. Other CD-ROM suppliers may specify a particular drive. To ease the drive requirements, the CD-ROM publisher may offer options to lease the disc or may even offer subscription rates that include lease charges for hardware (drive and/or microprocessor). Dialog's OnDisc MEDLINE, for example, uses the Philips CM-100 drive, which sells for $740. BRS's Colleague Disc offers options for using a Philips drive (at a purchase price of $930 or lease price of $575 per year). One MEDLINE CD-ROM product (Compact Med-Base) requires two CD-ROM drives.

Magnetic storage requirements also vary from product to product. Available hard disk capacity may be as great as three megabytes.

Scope

CD-ROM-based MEDLINE products vary considerably in the amount of MEDLINE coverage offered. Three basic variables are involved:

- the years covered
- the amount of MEDLINE coverage
- how contents are segmented among more than one CD

Many MEDLINE discs, such as Cambridge Scientific Abstracts' COM-PACT/MEDLINE, DIALOG's OnDisc MEDLINE, and BRS/Colleague Disc MEDLINE, are "annuals"—a single CD-ROM contains one year of MEDLINE data. Prior years are available and may be "packaged" into archival sets or as part of a current subscription.

Dialog has three subscription rates: (1) $960 for one CD-ROM disc containing the current year; (2) $1,450 for two CD-ROM discs, one containing the current year and the second containing the previous year's entries; and (3) $2,450 for five discs, covering the current year plus the four previous years.

Cambridge Scientific Abstracts offers the current annual at one subscription rate (of $975), archival CD-ROM discs of individual years from 1984 at a reduced rate of $750 each, and for $3,000 a set of four CD-ROM discs archiving MEDLINE listings from 1983 through 1986.

BRS Information Technologies charges $995 to subscribe to the current year and offers the 1988 disc plus the 1987 disc for $1,650. (Years prior to 1987 are not yet offered on CD-ROM disc from BRS.)

SilverPlatter charges $2,500 for a five-year set.

By selecting only portions of MEDLINE, some CD-ROM publishers of MEDLINE listings can fit more years of data onto each disc.

Aries's MEDLINE Knowledge Finder has a subset of MEDLINE citations, listing articles from 225 major biomedical journals over a five-year period. Each citation is in an unabridged form.

EBSCO Electronic Information has two MEDLINE subsets. Its Core MEDLINE contains the current and two previous years of citations of Priority 1 Journals (an abridged Index Medicus) and Special Lists of the Nursing and Dentistry databases, covering 552 titles (versus the 3,000+ titles cited in MEDLINE). EBSCO has numerous pricing options (frequency of updates, monthly or annual billing, duration of subscriptions with discount beyond the 12-month minimum, lease of CD-ROM drive, etc.) which factor into the price of its CD-ROM discs. The Core MEDLINE compact disc subscriptions range from $799 to $1,795 with drive.

EBSCO's Comprehensive MEDLINE, with the current and two previous years of all the journals of Core MEDLINE plus English-language Priority 2 Journals (an abridged Index Medicus), covers 2,000 titles and requires two discs. The annual subscription for Comprehensive MEDLINE ranges from $1,649 to $2,995 with CD-ROM drive.

Digital Diagnostics, Inc.'s BiblioMed contains only specific MEDLINE entries selected by physicians at Johns Hopkins Hosptial and the Mayo Clinic, based on perceived usefulness to practicing physicians.

Most comprehensive is Online Research Systems' Compact Med-Base. It is a nine-disc set, covering the 23 years of the entire MEDLINE database. A single CD-ROM disc contains five to seven years of MEDLINE. After using a disc to locate desired records, the appropriate second disc containing the complete abstract is loaded into the dual-drive system. The company has used special data compression techniques that allow for searching of five years of the database and as many as 1.5 million records at one time. Subscriptions are $3,495 per year.

Especially for searchers used to online databases of infinite size, with no segmentation by year of publication, the more years that can be searched at once the better. Since many CD-ROM discs currently require rebooting the system when changing from one disc to another, the searcher may have to go through several extra steps to locate related records from years other than the year(s) contained on the CD-ROM disc in use. Likewise, some searchers may not wish to restrict themselves to only a portion of the MEDLINE database. Abridged citations may not be acceptable in some situations. Some users may be content with citations from English-language-only publications, or Priority 1/Special Lists, or an even smaller subset of journals. Individuals view differently the trade-off of the number of journals against the number of years cited on the CD-ROM's database.

Frequency of Updates

About 25,000 citations are added to MEDLINE monthly. Online versions of MEDLINE can reflect these changes quickly, whereas CD-ROM updates require creating and distributing new discs. The majority of CD-ROM publishers supply updated versions quarterly. BRS updates its MEDLINE CD-ROM only three times a year (April, August, and December). This means an information seeker must supplement searches for articles published more recently (in the last three to five months) with printed or online bibliographies.

In response to the need for more up-to-date referencing, Online Research Systems plans to update its Compact MedBase Online monthly. EBSCO has also announced plans to offer both quarterly and monthly updates of Core MEDLINE and Comprehensive MEDLINE.

The Orientation of the CD-ROM Publisher

CD-ROM publishers that also offer online bibliographic databases are likely to maintain the same searching techniques for both databases, providing compatibility for searchers who use both and are already familiar with their respective online techniques. Publishers may also add some special features for less experienced searchers.

DIALOG and BRS are two information providers that publish both online and CD-ROM versions of MEDLINE. BRS searching with CD-ROM is automatically simpler since the user does not have to specify languages (only English-language articles are offered) or time span (since only one year is contained on a disc). But while the CD-ROM version uses the more "user-friendly" BRS/Colleague searching prompts and software (versus BRS/Search software), there are few menus and no special features for the novice. To use the CD-ROM effectively, the searcher must know (or learn) Boolean logic and BRS/Colleague search functions and commands.

In contrast, DIALOG offers two methods of searching its CD-ROM version of MEDLINE. In addition to the standard command language

Figure 9. DIALOG OnDisc. Courtesy Dialog Information Services, Inc.

method used by experienced searchers for accessing its online version, DIALOG offers its "Easy Menu." With its menu orientation and numerous helps (displaying truncated words with variants, displaying variants for an author search, a color screen, easy thesaurus access), a novice does not need training or a skilled search intermediary in order to develop search strategies and alternative strategies and to print or download search results. There are drawbacks to using the Easy Menu versus using the command language, such as the need to restep through each menu to change the search strategy, the inability to capture a search history, and the inability to save a search strategy to use on another disc (year) of MEDLINE. DIALOG has added some extra features that are not found in its online offering, such as programming of function keys (for single-key commands) and the ability to sort the results of a search in sequence by author, date, or journal.

Other CD-ROM publishers such as Online Research Systems, EBSCO, and Cambridge Scientific that also offer online products but not an online version of MEDLINE, have developed specialized, proprietary software for using their CD-ROM versions of MEDLINE.

Cambridge Scientific Abstracts, which also offers various scientific online databases, opted to use search techniques that differ from its online searching methods. For searching its COMPACT MEDLINE, two levels of searching are available. The menu-driven novice level takes the searcher through establishing the search argument by a series of detailed menus. The menus, however, do not provide for all the nuances of searching MEDLINE, such as placing hyphens between MeSH headings for multi-word searches and placing a colon at the end of a MeSH term to locate all occurrences of the term. The interactive command level requires the knowledge of an experienced searcher. However, regardless of the level used to establish the search criteria, the system searches the database in the same way, searching by words, parts of words, by Boolean operators, by proximity operators, and by truncation. Help screens, dictionary displays (to verify search terms), and options for displaying/saving/printing searching strategies and results exist at both levels.

Online Research Systems is building on its online expertise to help differentiate its MEDLINE disc. In addition to the 23-year coverage and monthly updates, its Compact Med-Base also has novice and expert modes for searching. It offers some special aids for working with MeSH terms, such as mapping "free-text" (non-MeSH) words to the MeSH nomenclature, explaining and displaying MeSH hierarchies, and referencing permuted MeSH terms. Furthermore, for those already familiar with NLM's or BRS's online searching commands, it allows using those search commands at both the novice and expert levels.

SilverPlatter's background is different from that of online publishers. As a developer of numerous CD-ROM products on various topics, the company is oriented toward developing products that are compatible with its other CD-ROM discs. Search commands for its MEDLINE disc are similar to searching commands on its other CD-ROM databases. Its software includes extensive on-screen helps, including how to change discs, tutorials on system functions, and searching with MeSH terms. It also allows searching with MeSH terms without knowing the MeSH abbreviations. Compatibility trade-offs, or perhaps lack of online bibliographic experience, may account for certain limitations, such as the inability to display or print anything other than the last result of a search argument.

For CD-ROM publishers that don't have any compatibility requirements with their other online or CD-ROM products, software can explore different options, especially to meet market needs. Aries, with its Knowledge Finder, is obviously focusing attention on the novice searcher. This Macintosh-based system will seem less forbidding to someone unfamiliar with microcomputers. Its menus guide the novice through establishing search requests and disc handling. It will map free-text words to MeSH's specific terminology. And while its MEDLINE CD-ROM has citations from only 225 journals, citations are unabridged and many include abstracts. The limited scope of journals may be less acceptable to an intermediary searcher, while the novice may be more comfortable with the selections and availability of abstracts.

Figure 10. Before using Knowledge Finder, the user must acknowledge copyright obligations associated with the database and its use. Courtesy Aries Systems Corporation.

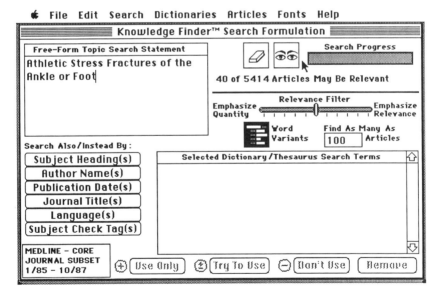

Figure 11. Knowledge Finder allows the user to create a sentence-style search statement, and requires no command language. In addition, any number of terms may be added to the search formulation, using the dictionaries or thesaurus. Courtesy Aries Systems Corporation.

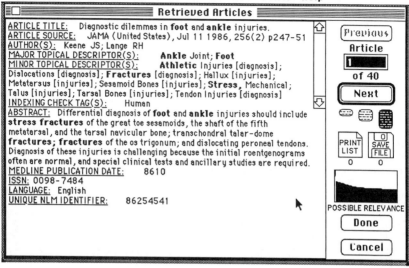

Figure 12. Retrieved article citations are viewed in order of likely relevance, based upon an analysis of the user's search statement. Any one of three display formats can be used. Courtesy Aries Systems Corporation.

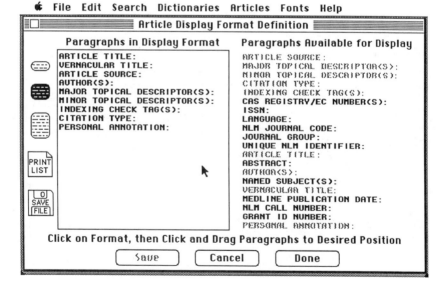

Figure 13. The user can set the content and sequence of any of the screen display, printing, or save-to-disk formats. Intuitive pointing, clicking, and dragging of citation fields allows easy and rapid redesign of citation layouts. Courtesy Aries Systems Corporation.

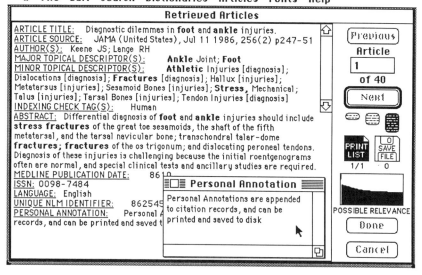

Figure 14. Personal Annotations can be added to any citation, which are then printed or saved to disk with the citation. Courtesy Aries Systems Corporation.

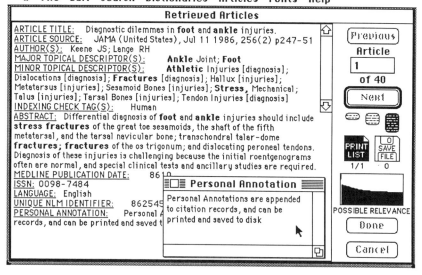

Figure 15. If a search word is not found in Knowledge Finder's word dictionary, neighboring alternatives are suggested. When the user selects an alternative, the replacement word is placed automatically into the search statement, and the search is resumed. Courtesy Aries Systems Corporation.

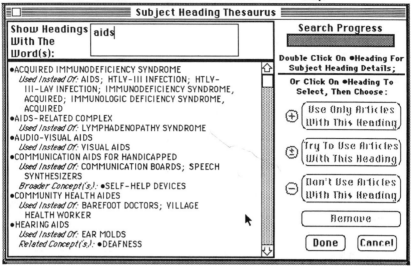

Figure 16. The Medical Subject Heading Thesaurus identifies all index terms that can be applied to article citations. Courtesy Aries Systems Corporation.

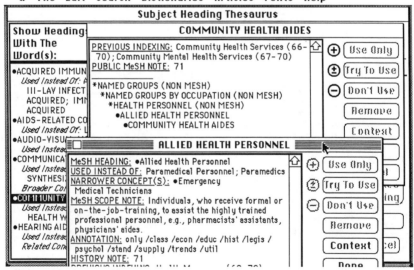

Figure 17. Details for any subject heading can be displayed, using hypertext-style navigation through the Thesaurus database. Subject heading hierarchies drawn from the Thesaurus suggest broader and narrower concepts that may be appropriate for the search. Courtesy Aries Systems Corporation.

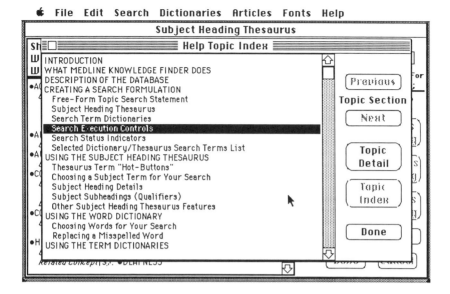

Figure 18. The on-screen Help tools provide context-sensitive assistance when using Knowledge Finder. Most of the hard-copy documentation is incorporated into the Help facility. Courtesy Aries Systems Corporation.

CD-ROM Versus Online

The CD-ROM versions of MEDLINE, when compared to the online versions, are usually evaluated according to the needs and experiences of expert searchers and intermediaries. For that level, ease-of-use is less important than the richness of the command language and the speed of locating articles with complex search arguments. Especially considering the time pressures associated with online searching, such evaluation criteria is understandable. If the goal of a MEDLINE disc is to allow the information seeker to do searches without an intermediary, ease-of-use issues become quite important. Speed factors become less important since the user is not paying an expensive penalty for online "connect time."

In comparison with online versions, CD-ROM versions of MEDLINE are easier for a novice to use. Most of the current MEDLINE discs offer some "user-friendly" features. And by virtue of no "meter ticking," responding to menus and experimenting can proceed at a more leisurely pace. Yet most of the MEDLINE discs do not go far enough. As Donna Lee and Joanna Weinstock reported in their recent study of the BRS Colleague Disc, selected CD-ROM versions could yield identical search results to online counterparts, but only if MeSH terms were used. Few MEDLINE discs offer sufficient help with MeSH vocabulary.

At the novice level, the inability to save previous searches and search histories is not especially user-friendly. Only at the expert level can these be accommodated as they are with online versions.

Especially "unfriendly" is the need to swap CD-ROM discs in order to search a broad time frame of biomedical publications.

When using discs, a searcher would also need to check an online version for articles that have been published in the last one to four months.

In addition, there are some special limitations compared to online versions, such as the ability for only one person to use the database at one time; potential downtime for hardware malfunctions; and potential security issues (such as someone walking away with the disc). The more positive aspects of these CD-ROM discs are their fixed costs, reduced training requirements for use, special features offered on selected discs, and the opportunity for the end-user to conduct searches without an intermediary.

Trends and Forecasts

The discussion of MEDLINE discs has highlighted various issues, some of which are specific to the bibliographic nature of the material. It also illustrated the importance of software in a CD-ROM product.

More software developments are needed to create information systems that fit the needs and expertise of the user. "Expert systems" and development of more hypertext features will help. Evolving natural query languages may be less important than in other industries. Since the science and health care fields use very precise terminology, mapping software and techniques other than online methods and Boolean searches may be more appropriate. Using a results list for browsing and "an expanding table of contents," allowing the user to peruse the contents of the disc and dynamically expand contents sections, lets the user apply print-oriented skills to the process. Features such as pop-up windows, a mouse, and a color screen can help the user work more comfortably with electronic information systems. Most important is providing the information user with an information tool that is intuitively understood and mastered, and that has obvious advantages over the seeker's current methods. At the same time, the "friendliness" of the system must not jeopardize the power of the system to quickly and comprehensively supply necessary information.

With the ongoing requirements for information in science and health care, there is a need for better information access. Besides creating easily mastered, friendly systems, several aspects need further development.

More full-text anthologies ("knowledge bases") on specific topics are needed. COMPACT LIBRARY: AIDS, for example, offers in-depth full-text information in a very compact, easily referenced form. When limited in subject matter, the user has not only bibliographic references, but also immediate access to the actual text without online expenses or additional steps or delays to obtain desired articles. More and more discs focused on a specific topic can be expected.

Distribution of graphic data, such as still and motion color images that illustrate characteristics (and symptoms), and processes that allow various perspectives and close-ups, in conjunction with textual data, are areas of potential development.

Users can expect more creative use of audio and visual techniques to create reference and education materials for lay persons such as patients.

One can look forward to the creation of more hybrid systems where the CD-ROM works together with several other components to provide integrated information systems that meet the user's requirements and environment (e.g., videodisc simulations with textual CD-ROM discs).

Summary

Currently there are more than 50 CD-ROM titles in the scientific, medical, and health care fields. The majority are used in institutional settings, such as hospitals, libraries, and research organizations. Even one of the most successful CD-ROM series, Micromedex's Computerized Clinical Information System, used in hospital emergency rooms, poison control centers, drug information centers, and pharmacies, is being used by only 20 percent of the 1,500 sites that have used the microfilm version of the product. In library settings, CD-ROM discs are generally viewed as supplements, rather than substitutes, for online and print versions of products.

When the needed developments outlined in the last section occur, we should begin to see products that are more suitable, targeted, and desirable for scientists and health care professionals. Given their enormous information needs, they will be most responsive to products that meet their needs and can intuitively be mastered. The majority of CD-ROM discs in science and health care today are focused on replicating and enhancing online products. Thus, many lack the features to attract a broad base of individual information seekers. Instead, developers in these fields that wish to attract a broad base of users— beyond the information intermediaries and computer-literate professionals—need to focus on developing desktop knowledge bases that have the power of online searching, immediate access to actual data, and applications software that is appealing to use.

References

Desmarais, Norman. "Information Management on a Compact Silver Disc." *Optical Information Systems* 7:3 (May/June 1987): 193-201. Meckler Corporation, Westport, CT.
Duggan, Mary Kay. "A Look at Dialog's First CD-ROM Product." *Optical Information Systems* 7:6 (November/December 1987): 401-405. Meckler Corporation, Westport, CT.
Kuchta, Nancy E., and Winokur, Marilyn G. "Budgeting and Marketing: The Micromedex Project." *CD-ROM Review* 2:5 (November/December 1987): 35-37. CW Communications, Peterborough, NH.
Lee, Donna, and Weinstock, Joanna. "BRS Colleague Disc." *CD-ROM Librarian* (February 1988): 32-39. Meckler Corporation, Westport, CT.
March, Bob. "Hypertext (minus the Hype)." Speech at Seybold Seminars, San Francisco, March 8, 1988.
Nelson, Nancy Melin, ed. "MEDLINE CD-ROM on a Macintosh." *CD-ROM Librarian* (September/October 1987): 8. Meckler Corporation, Westport, CT.
Nelson, Nancy Melin, ed. *CD-ROM Librarian* (July/August 1987). Meckler Corporation, Westport, CT.
Nelson, Nancy Melin. *CD-ROMs in Print, 1987.* Meckler Corporation, Westport, CT.
O'Connor, Mary Ann, ed. *Optical Information Systems Update* 7:4 (March 15, 1988). Meckler Corporation, Westport, CT.
Tiampo, Janet. "CD-ROM Disc Titles." *CD-ROM Review* 3:2 (March/April 1988): 54-65. CW Communications, Peterborough, NH.
Zeichick, Alan L. "In the Name of Science." *CD-ROM Review* 3:1 (January/February 1988): 52-53. CW Communications, Peterborough, NH.

Appendix A: MEDLINE CD-ROMs (according to title)

BiblioMed
Digital Diagnostics Inc.
601 University Avenue, Suite 255
Sacramento, CA 95825
916-921-6629

BRS/Colleague Disc—MEDLINE
BRS Information Technologies
555 East Lancaster Avenue, 4th floor
Saint David, PA 19087
800-468-0908

COMPACT/Cambridge MEDLINE
Cambridge Scientific Abstracts
5161 River Road
Bethesda, MD 20816
301-951-1400

Compact Med-Base
Online Research Systems
2901 Broadway, Suite 154
New York, NY 10025
212-408-3311

Core MEDLINE/EBSCO CD-ROM
EBSCO Electronic Information
P.O. Box 13787
Torrance, CA 90503
213-530-7533

Comprehensive MEDLINE/EBSCO CD-ROM
EBSCO Electronic Information
P.O. Box 13787
Torrance, CA 90503
213-530-7533

DIALOG OnDisc MEDLINE
DIALOG Information Services
3460 Hillview Avenue
Palo Alto, CA 94394
800-3-DIALOG

MEDLINE Knowledge Finder
Aries Systems Corporation
79 Boxford Street
North Andover, MA 01845
617-689-9334

MEDLINE on SilverPlatter
SilverPlatter Information Inc.
37 Walnut Street
Wellesley Hills, MA 02181
617-239-0306

Appendix B: Other CD-ROMs Mentioned in Chapter
(according to company)

Robotics database (under development)
AIRS, Inc.
335 Paint Branch Drive
College Park, MD   20742
301-454-2022

ASFA Aquatic Science & Fisheries and
Life Sciences 1/83 to 8/85
Cambridge Scientific Abstracts
5161 River Road
Bethesda, MD 20816
301-951-1400

Ccinfodisc
CCOHS
250 Main Street East
Hamilton ONT L8N 1H6
Canada
416-572-2981

The Physician Library
The Nurse Library
Ellis Enterprises, Inc.
225 N.W. Thirteenth Street
Oklahoma City, OK   73103
405-235-7660

ca-CD (Cancer Abstracts)
Elsevier
52 Vanderbilt Avenue
New York, NY 10017
212-370-5520

CD/Biotech
IASC/PC-SIG
1040E East Duane
Sunnyvale, CA 94086
408-730-9291

Science Citation Index
Institute for Scientific Information
3501 Market Street
Philadelphia, PA 19104
215-386-0100

Powder Diffraction File
Int'l Center for Diffraction Data
2602 Park Lane
Swarthmore, PA 19801
215-328-9400

ADONIS CD-ROM Biomedical Collection
IOD
P.O. Box 1370
Berkeley, CA 94701
800-227-7500
415-644-4500

Oncodisc
J.P. Lippincott Co., Inc.
East Washington Square
Philadelphia, PA 19105
215-238-4200

McGraw-Hill CD-ROM Science & Technical Reference Set
McGraw-Hill Book Company
11 West 19th Street
New York, NY 10011
212-512-2000

COMPACT LIBRARY: AIDS
Medical Publishing Group
1440 Main Street
Waltham, MA 02154
617-893-3800

Drugdex
Emerindex
Identidex Poisindex
Micromedex Inc.
6600 Bannock Street, Suite 350
Denver, CO 80204
303-623-8600

OHS MSDS on Disc
Occupation Health Services
450 Seventh Avenue, Suite 2407
New York, NY 10123
212-967-1100

AGRICOLA
NTIS
OCLC
6565 Frantz Road
Dublin, OH 43017
614-764-6000

Two collections of planetary science data
(from Univ. of Colorado's Laboratory for Atmospheric and
Space Physics)
Reference Technology Inc.
5700 Flatiron Parkway
Boulder, CO 80301
303-449-4157

AGRICOLA/Cain
Cancer-CD
Chem-Bank
NTIS (five titles in series)
OSH-ROM (Niosh, Hseline & Cisdoc)
PyscLIT
Sociofile
SilverPlatter Information Inc.
37 Walnut Street
Wellesley Hills, MA 02181
617-239-0306

Data Archive on Adolescent Pregnancy & Pregnancy Prevention
Sociometrics Corporation
685 High Street, 2E
Palo Alto, CA 94301
415-321-7846

Voyager II Images of Uranus, Vol. 1
Univ. of Colo. LASP
Campus Bos B10
Boulder, CO 80309
303-492-6867

National Meteorological Grid Point Data Set and
Gale Experiment Set
University of Washington Dept. of Atmospheric Sciences
Seattle, WA 98195
206-545-0910

CD-ROM Prototype Disc
U.S. Geological Survey
804 National Center
Reston, VA 22092
703-648-4000

The Intl Dictionary of Medicine & Biology
Kirk-Othermer Encyl. of Chemical Technology
Mark Encyl. of Polymer Science & Engineering
Registry of Mass Spectral Data
John Wiley & Sons
605 Third Avenue
New York, NY 10158
212-850-6000

Applied Science & Technology Index
General Science Index
Social Sciences Index
H.W. Wilson Co.
950 University Avenue
Bronx, NY 10452
212-588-8400

3
Government and Law

NORMAN DESMARAIS

This chapter focuses on CD-ROM applications in the government and legal markets. Rather than discuss applications by the types of information that they contain (e.g., bibliographic, statistical, graphic), this chapter is organized according to the various agencies that provide the source data for CD-ROM. Since very few agencies produce their own CD-ROMs, most of the CD-ROM discs used by the U.S. government have been developed by private vendors based on the information products gathered and produced by the same government agencies.

The government's role as an information provider is briefly explored, as are some possible reasons that the government has not yet wholeheartedly embraced CD-ROM for data distribution. After examining how vendors obtain the rights to use this data and fill this vacuum, applications in the various national libraries (Library of Congress, National Library of Medicine, National Agricultural Library) and bibliographic databases available from other agencies (Government Printing Office [GPO] and the National Technical Information Service [NTIS]) will be discussed. Also, this chapter addresses some statistical applications such as those provided by the Securities and Exchange Commission and the Bureau of the Census. Graphics databases for maps (U.S. Geological Survey), some of which combine statistical data, will be described along with applications at the Department of Defense.

The second section of this chapter focuses on legal applications. In the legal market there are two major thrusts which are not mutually exclusive: library applications and those for practicing attorneys (i.e., bibliographic and full-text products). Although legal libraries may proceed at the same pace as their academic counterparts, lawyers hesitate to adopt the new technology. CD-ROM vendors may have to form coalitions or subdivide the profession into several sub-specialties (vertical markets) in order to make any sales or to survive in this environment.

Government

The U.S. government, through its various agencies, constitutes the country's largest single producer of information. To keep from drowning in the flood of paper they produce and handle, some departments have actively engaged in researching cost-effective methods of mass storage of text and data. Optical information system technology seems to offer a solution to this problem. While write-once, read many (WORM) technology seems more appropriate for internal use with limited distribution, CD-ROM offers a better alternative for external use and mass distribution.

The government has often assumed a leadership role in sponsoring and encouraging scientific research. However, with few exceptions, it has not assumed such a role with optical storage. The high costs of research and development, preparing, mastering, and producing discs may provide one deterrent to their broad application throughout the government. A major factor affecting the government's application is the lack of software standards that prohibit the transportability of CD-ROM discs and their compatibility with different hardware systems in different agencies. Another significant reason is the small base of installed equipment to use such products effectively, both in the private and public sectors.

Because tax revenues support the gathering and publication of all the information produced by the government, most of these funds support information dissemination in the public domain (with the exception of classified or secret information needed for defense or national security). Thus, the government provides an opportunity for entrepreneurs and information brokers to obtain some large databases quite inexpensively to test and develop CD-ROM products. With the government apparently reluctant to assume a leadership role in the development and application of CD-ROM technology, information entrepreneurs have jumped at the opportunity.

While the government publishes data in traditional formats (often available free or at nominal cost from the Government Printing Office or NTIS), several firms produce value-added equivalents on CD-ROM. While many purchasers may object to paying for information that they can obtain at little or no cost, database vendors respond that subscribers receive the added value that permits them to increase productivity, decrease labor costs, and store the information itself in a variety of ways. Advantages include the reduction of search time or elimination of intermediary searching, decrease in online costs for frequently used databases while maintaining a fixed-price subscription, and savings in space and storage costs. CD-ROM discs also help to maximize control over information products by providing additional access points. Discs that include full-text eliminate the need to use cumbersome and difficult-to-use information storage formats such as microform. They also do away with filing errors that obstruct retrieval, thereby saving the personnel costs associated with maintaining information collections.

While few government agencies are actively involved in producing their own data on CD-ROM, many are early adopters of the technology and collaborate with the information providers, thereby maximizing the products' effectiveness for their purposes.

CD-ROM providers can obtain several databases from the NTIS by securing a license from it and paying fees for the computer magnetic tapes. For databases not available from the NTIS, vendors must negotiate permission with each individual agency.

Although a government agency may occasionally approach a CD-ROM provider, the vendor usually approaches the agency to obtain the right to use its database. Some agencies are more possessive of their databases than others and are reluctant to allow CD-ROM access. Government agencies may soon approach vendors to produce their databases as CD-ROM technology is more widely understood, familiar, and stable as an information tool. After negotiating license agreements, the two parties sign contracts. Although these contracts varied from agency to agency in the beginning of CD-ROM product development, they are now becoming more standardized. The database vendor usually prefers that the agency review the work before actual disc distribution. Some agencies such as the National Library of Medicine insist on this and have a sign-off right to ensure consistent quality among the various forms of its product.

While CD-ROM technology offers the federal government advantages in distributing information to depository libraries, many of them are technology-poor and do not have the required retrieval systems. Now that drives (Amdek/Hitachi) and discs (Microsoft's Bookshelf) are appearing in retail outlets such as Sears and Radio Shack, prices should begin to fall due to increased competition. Consequently, the educated consumer will gradually recognize CD-ROM and its value. It appears only a matter of time before the CD-ROM drive becomes a necessity for a PC workstation in order to meet demands for information in the government market.

Library of Congress (LC)

The Library of Congress has assumed a leadership role in the exploration of all optical media for data storage and ranks among the early adopters. It has produced bibliographic records in machine readable form (MARC) since 1968 and had a large and very active database when optical storage media appeared on the scene. Since the nation's libraries rely on this data to expedite cataloging most of their materials, they have constituted a primary market for CD-ROM products. LC's MARC database has presented an ideal opportunity to test the market for bibliographic records in CD-ROM format.

Early products such as Information Access Company's InfoTrac and Library Systems and Services' MiniMARC used videodiscs that have not had much success in the library market. CD-ROM versions have proved considerably more successful. The Library Corporation paved the way with its BiblioFile Cataloging Production Module which includes MARC records for books, GPO publications, music, films, maps, and Canadian publications. Other companies such as General Research Corporation, Library Systems and Services, a division of Gaylord Brothers, and OCLC (Online Computer Library Center) soon followed The Library Corporation's example.[1] (See Chapter 1 for a discussion of these and other related CD-ROM applications.)

In addition to providing a convenient distribution medium for such a large quantity of data, CD-ROM has facilitated bibliographic searching and effected great time savings by eliminating much duplication of effort in cataloging library materials. Local libraries, recognizing the power of the medium, have developed custom CD-ROM discs for their own public-access catalogs and union catalogs.

The Library of Congress's Cataloging Distribution Service (CDS), working with Online Computer Systems, Inc. on a Disc Distribution Pilot Project, will provide MARC bibliographic and/or authority records via CD-ROM disc to internal LC users and/or end-user libraries outside LC.

Government Printing Office (GPO)

The various CD-ROM versions of the GPO's Monthly Catalog have facilitated the identification of numerous government publications. While the printed versions include a variety of indices, the average person finds them difficult to use. Interestingly, reference and government documents librarians report that the adoption of CD-ROM has led to an increase in demand for and use of government publications. The large amount of space needed to store these documents presents a problem to government library depositories. CD-ROM technology helps to decrease space requirements and the related storage costs. One report estimates that it costs between two and five cents to store a megabyte of data on CD-ROM compared to $5 to $7 for paper storage.[2] Analysts have also determined that CD-ROM provides the most cost-effective method of storage compared to other optical media (including hardware costs), thus producing the maximum savings per information file.

Many documents come as single sheets or pamphlets which are easily lost. A great amount of labor is required to catalog and file these items properly and to maintain such collections for proper access for future use. To produce the economies required by the Gramm-

Rudman-Hollings Act, the GPO has decreased the number of publications and increased the use of microforms. Thus, an information user must search at least two locations to locate a document. In addition to facilitating searching and minimizing space requirements, CD-ROM storage makes it easier to locate and use these items. For example, Microsoft has addressed this problem for business publications with its Small Business Consultant which includes more than 220 government publications. This CD-ROM product helps small business owners obtain the information necessary to start and operate a business.

Reference and government documents librarians receive many requests for government statistics, especially for those in the *Statistical Abstract of the United States*. Often the user finds it difficult to locate the data in a useful form. Microsoft's newest CD-ROM product, Stat-Pack, offers a solution by compiling official U.S. government facts and figures on the economy, politics, demographics, manufacturing, industry, trade, agriculture, and business. It includes the *Statistical Abstract of the United States, U.S. Business Statistics,* and *Agricultural Statistics.* Compatibility with popular word processing and spreadsheet programs eliminates the need to rekey the data.

Libraries and depositories often intimidate users by the large quantities of information stored and the cumbersome methods of retrieving relevant selections. When looking for a needle in the haystack, the user wants to find the needle—not the haystack—and CD-ROM can help locate it. Facilitating an information audit can open depositories to new constituencies that either do not know what is stored in a depository library or are put off because it takes too much effort to identify which documents contain the needed data. After the identification process, some information users may get frustrated when they cannot locate the data in a usable form or in a given depository.

The GPO's Union List of Item Selections would be useful on CD-ROM. This publication helps to locate documents held by other depositories through the item number. While the GPO can produce a national list, it claims it cannot (or will not) produce regional ones that would often be more useful. A CD-ROM version of this title could accommodate such requests.

National Library of Medicine (NLM)

The National Library of Medicine has signed several collaborative, experimental agreements allowing commercial firms to choose any segment of MEDLINE to put on CD-ROM or to offer MEDLINE records with other data with NLM's approval. While all products will initially contain MEDLINE data, we can assume that they will eventually include other MEDLARS databases. Vendors include: BRS Information

Technologies (BRS/Colleague Disc), The Faxon Company (MEDLINE Knowledge Finder developed by Aries Systems Corporation to run on the Apple Macintosh), DIALOG Information Services, Inc. (part of the DIALOG OnDisc family), OCLC (Search CD450 family), SilverPlatter Information, Inc., Digital Diagnostics (BiblioMed), and Cambridge Scientific Abstracts (Compact Cambridge which includes the Life Sciences Collection as well as MEDLINE). Each of these products targets specific users. Some serve practicing physicians, health care providers, and hospital personnel. Others are designed for libraries, researchers, or students. Together, these CD-ROM products offer purchasers the widest selection of search software features and options of any CD-ROM database.

Medically related products based on information provided by government agencies include the International Association for Scientific Computing's CD/Biotech, SilverPlatter's OSH-ROM and Chem-bank, as well as Knowledge Access International's NATASHA. CD/Biotech includes Genbank (the Genetic Sequences Databank sponsored by the National Institute of Health), the National Biomedical Research Foundation's Protein Identification Resource, and the European Molecular Biology Laboratory's Data Library.

OSH-ROM includes information from NIOSHTIC, produced by the National Institute for Occupational Safety and Health; HSELINE, produced by Health and Safety Executive, Library and Information Services in the United Kingdom; and CISDOC, produced by the International Labour Office of the International Occupational Safety and Health Information Centre in Geneva.

Chem-bank combines RTECS, the Registry of Toxic Effects of Chemical Substances, from the National Institute for Occupational Safety and Health; CHRIS, Chemical Hazard Response Information System, from the U.S. Department of Transportation; and OHMTADS, Oil and Hazardous Materials-Technical Assistance Data, from the U.S. Environmental Protection Agency.

Knowledge Access International has produced a CD-ROM version of Sociometrics Corporation's *Data Archive on Adolescent Pregnancy and Pregnancy Prevention* which the U.S. Office of Population Affairs sponsors under contract to Sociometrics. Entitled NATASHA: National Archive On Sexuality, Health, & Adolescence, it provides instant access to more than 109 data sets and 39,793 variables from 82 major studies relevant to adolescent fertility. Dr. Matilda Butler, president of Knowledge Access International, believes that "the real value of any new technology is applications that have the potential of bringing about social or economic change." This product aims to help social scientists, social workers, and health professionals obtain information that will help them solve teenage pregnancy problems.

National Agricultural Library (NAL)

AGRICOLA (AGRICultural OnLine Access), available through SilverPlatter and OCLC, provides bibliographic citations relating to all aspects of agriculture. Produced by the Science and Education Administration, Technical Information Systems (SEA/TIS) of the U.S. Department of Agriculture, AGRICOLA serves as the document locator and bibliographic control system for the SEA/TIS collection. The National Agricultural Library draws on it to print cards for its catalogs. While the OCLC product offers retrospective discs going back to 1979, Silver-Platter's retrospective includes CAIN (AGRICOLA's predecessor) going back to 1970. OCLC also enhances its product with Agriculture Materials in Libraries (AgMIL) which contains MARC records from its online union catalog in the area of agriculture. Its three discs cover computers, environment, and energy.

National Technical Information Service (NTIS)

The National Technical Information Service brokers much of the government's technical data to the public. Users can search its database online through a variety of databanks to identify government-sponsored research, development, engineering reports and analyses prepared by federal agencies, their contractors, and grantees. The database also contains abstracts of unclassified, publicly available reports, software packages, and data files from 300 government agencies. The NTIS will also fill orders for hard copies of each document. DIALOG Information Services, Inc., SilverPlatter Information, Inc., and OCLC have produced subsets of the NTIS database.

The efforts to privatize the NTIS, along with other government agencies, could affect the availability of technical information to the public. Government agencies will be more reluctant to provide private companies with documents. We can expect prices of items now available at nominal cost to increase as private firms attempt to make a profit. By the same token, a private company will decrease or eliminate its stock of slow-selling material, further limiting access. The NTIS databases (both online and on disc) that provide bibliographic citations would also diminish in coverage and increase in cost because they depend on the availability of these documents. The impact on the quality of the end product depends on several factors that nobody can predict at this time. Some experts expect the quality and service to improve; others anticipate its deterioration.

With several companies marketing different offerings of the same database, purchasers have a wider choice of search and retrieval software, user interfaces, software options and utilities, as well as content (subsets of the main database or the entire file). For example, OCLC enhances all its products with records from its online union catalog corresponding to the subject area of the particular database.

Securities and Exchange Commission (SEC)

Unlike databases produced directly by government agencies, the Disclosure/Spectrum Stock Ownership Database (Compact Disclosure) depends on data that the SEC collects in the form of quarterly and annual reports, 10K, 10Q statements, etc., from publicly owned companies and makes available to the public. While Compact Disclosure may come to mind as the primary source of this financial data on CD-ROM, other versions appear in Lotus Development Corporation's One Source and Datext Inc.'s (now owned by Lotus) CD/Corporate discs.

U.S. Postal Service (USPS)

Another database that has found its way into a variety of products (such as ERIC, MEDLINE, AGRICOLA, and NTIS) is the National Postal Service Directory. Information Design Incorporated (IDI) has stored the entire 47 volumes on a single CD-ROM disc called the Address Verification System Plus (AVS+). Users can retrieve any U.S. address along with its ZIP + 4 code in less than two seconds. ALDE Publishing, a subsidiary of TMS, Inc., also has a version called the ZIP + 4 Directory as does Omni Computer Systems, Inc. (Flash + 4). Microsoft's Bookshelf integrates the five-digit codes with several writer's tools.

U.S. Bureau of the Census

Statistics present a type of application particularly suited to the storage capacity and retrieval capabilities of CD-ROM. In addition to providing random access to specific data elements, most CD-ROM products interface with popular spreadsheet programs, allowing users to download and manipulate data as well as add user-specific data for comparison.

The U.S. Bureau of the Census has been evaluating CD-ROM technology as a means of distributing some of the large quantities of data it collects. The Bureau has already migrated from paper to microform and computer tape to distribute its immense quantity of data. CD-ROM seems a logical next choice. Recognizing the significance of census data to libraries and the fact that CD-ROM is rapidly becoming a significant method of electronic dissemination of information, the Bureau plans to release its Census Test Disc #2 shortly. It will contain data from the 1982 Census of Retail Trade by zip code and 1982 Census of Agriculture data by county for distribution to all depository libraries.

The Bureau of the Census will not provide hardware along with the disc, but the GPO hopes to provide support and advice to librarians who may be facing the new technology for the first time. The Bureau is considering the distribution of data from the next census on a CD-ROM disc.

Courtenay Slater, former chief economist for the U.S. Department of Commerce, and George Hall, former associate director of the Bureau of the Census, formed Slater Hall Information Products (SHIP) to market economic and social statistics on CD-ROM. These discs contain complete statistical files as released by the Census Bureau, the Bureau of Economic Analysis, and other federal statistical agencies. They also include definitions and documentation as prepared by the releasing agency. SHIP's first product covers the most recent Census of Agriculture: more than 3,000 data items for each county in the country—items such as number of farms, sales of selected agricultural products, total agricultural sales, and changes in the counties from 1978 to 1982.

SHIP's 1929-1986 Business Indicators CD-ROM contains three separate databases from the Bureau of Economic Analysis, U.S. Department of Commerce: complete GNP accounts from 1929 to 1986, business statistics, and income and employment figures by state and region. It includes 1,900 economic time series from the Commerce Department's "Blue Pages" in its monthly Survey of Current Business.

The firm's most recent product, County Statistics, includes more than 1,200 items of statistical information about each U.S. county, state, and metropolitan area. Data from the Census Bureau's COSTAT2 tape plus additional data on population, employment, and agriculture as well as totals for all metropolitan statistical areas, consolidated metropolitan areas, and primary metropolitan statistical areas are on this disc.

Subsequent CD-ROM discs will include such files as foreign trade statistics, employment statistics, personal income data, the census of U.S. manufacturers, resale and wholesale trade and services, and income and demographic data. The final selection will depend on the census bureau's update schedule and the timeliness of the data available.

General Services Administration (GSA)

The National Institute of Builders has produced several discs under the titles Building Sciences Information and Engineering Information Systems. The National Safety Data Corporation has mastered the Material Safety Data Sheets. Quantum Access, Inc. has a similar disc title: Material Safety Data System and Innovative Technology, another firm, has produced the Technical Logistics Reference Network on CD-ROM.

Information Handling Services's PERSONNET CD-ROM includes all of the major personnel databases and documents typically used by government personnel management organizations. It contains the entire Federal Personnel Manual and the full-text of significant documents from the Merit Systems Protection Board, the Federal Labor Relations Authority, and the Comptroller General.

U.S. Department of Customs

Reference Technology, Inc. has a subcontract from Electronic Data Systems for a field delivery system for the U.S. Department of Customs. The application will store 2,000 features of the faces of missing children as an aid to identification.

U.S. Geological Survey (USGS)

Many groups and firms such as land developers, political organizations, municipal and public utilities, and tax offices depend on map and geographic information to perform their work effectively. However, producing and updating this information in traditional paper formats is rather difficult and time consuming. CD-ROM represents significant savings over the expense of mainframe or online computer time and eliminates the need for expensive, trained programmer time.

The U.S. Geological Survey's National Earthquake Information Center has developed the Event CD to store earth science information—seismic readings of 5.5 magnitude and greater since 1929. As several universities request that the Center add them to its distribution list, the increased demand coupled with the planned increase in total volume of data (such as lowering the threshold of earthquake magnitude from 5.5 to 4.9 beginning with 1987 data, expanding the number of data collection sites, and including worldwide seismic arrays) has convinced the Center to change from magentic tape to CD-ROM.

The USGS also plans to produce other CD-ROM discs to store various types of geological information, Landsat images, digitized maps, etc., for easier access and manipulation with any software that runs under MS-DOS. CD-ROM's large-capacity storage permits easy access to data for purposes of examination or downloading to other software packages such as Lotus 1-2-3 for manipulation or analysis and subsequent inclusion in reports.

Geovision, Inc. is creating a library of maps (vector and raster data) and other types of graphic and geographic information on CD-ROM. Its GEOdisc family of products contains basic map images and related data for the continental United States based on satellite images and data from a multitude of government agencies, including the USGS (digital line graphs and digital elevation models), NOAA, EOSAT (Landsat), and the Bureau of the Census.

This firm aims to develop a complete PC-based geographic information system that allows periodic refreshment of data and permits the user to create, store, and maintain facility, boundary, or engineering records and graphics in an independent but totally compatible database. Its proprietary applications program, called "Windows/On The World," runs in the Microsoft "Windows" environment and permits the exchange of data between what is retrieved from the CD-ROM, and other applications such as word processors.

While first-generation CD-ROM discs include only map data, second-generation discs integrate census data with the maps. Chadwyck-Healey, Inc.'s Supermap includes the 1980 U.S. Census and digital mapping data on a single CD-ROM. The proprietary software allows the user to retrieve, manipulate, tabulate, rank, scan, and map information in up to 64 colors or monochrome. Furthermore, the software can accept user data and download to local software or data manipulators, such as Lotus 1-2-3.

The user extracts the data for mapping from retrieved tables, groups it into classes, and selects map colors and captions for each class. The system maps U.S. data onto prepared base maps for each state at the county level or for the whole country at the state level. The user can display the maps in a slow-motion sequence that enables the portrayal of changes in data through a time sequence or reflects comparative characteristics.

The firm's MUNDOCART/CD provides the same level of detail and search features for maps of the entire world. It includes coastlines with offshore islands, international and some administrative boundaries, major city and town boundaries, drainage systems (rivers, lakes, canals), and names of cities, towns, rivers, lakes, and islands. This CD-ROM product draws on the U.S. Defense Mapping Agency Operational Navigation Charts and the USSR Karta Mira series for Antarctica.

National Oceanic and Atmospheric Administration (NOAA)

The National Oceanic and Atmospheric Administration has developed a prototype CD-ROM disc to store selected historical weather data and to evaluate the technology's usefulness as a reference and teaching tool. If the experiment proves successful, the agency may store and distribute data from the Landsat satellite in this format. Various petroleum and timber companies use this imagery in mapping activities and for prospecting, thereby constituting a large market for the Landsat data. Transferring the database from magnetic tape to CD-ROM disc could simplify distribution of weather data to meteorologists and the military. Industries involved in exploration, construction, and other activities should also find a need for such a product.

Department of Defense (DoD)

CD-ROM also presents an ideal medium for the distribution of parts catalogs particularly to large populations such as the military. The National Standards Association has published a CD-ROM catalog entitled Parts Master (based on the National Stock Number System) for providers of products and services to the U.S. military and government purchasing departments. This product, based on the National Stock Number System, demonstrates how to correlate component identification in any of the systems used throughout the government to buy material. Complete information about the requirements of each of the 12 million parts acquired by the government is provided: shape, size, packaging, ratings, test data, etc. Some of the features include: NSN, FSC, FSCM, NSCM, IL's (Technical Characteristics), FSCNM, Military Part Numbers, and a few dozen other data fields and classes. This product consists of three discs, but the producer claims it is so easy to use that the documentation covers less than 30 pages.

While many government agencies have turned to CD-ROM to try to keep from drowning in the paper they either produce or collect, the Department of Defense is examining it as a means of maximizing military efficiency. Eliminating much of the paper in the filing cabinets in land-based offices as well as aboard warships (which could amount to more than 20 tons for a single Oliver Hazard Perry-class frigate, one of the Navy's smaller surface vessels) would permit stocking more ordnance or fuel. CD-ROM provides sailors with the technology to access needed information without inundating them with unusable formats. A single CD-ROM represents 12 gigabytes of data per pound. It also offers a medium of quick distribution of information; a disc can be shipped overnight anywhere in the country. However, it would take 29 and one-half days of continuous transmission to send the same data at 2400 baud over the telephone.

Obviously, military installations must be prepared to be self-contained in case of nuclear attack or for situations that require long periods of time without communication. Military units must have technical and maintenance manuals available to solve equipment problems on site. Very little space is available for storing the lengthy technical material that goes with the sophisticated equipment on military transports, tanks, ships, and aircraft.

Military applications do not often use off-the-shelf hardware, but there is a growing trend for doing so in non-combat environments. Usually, they require "militarized" equipment and weaponry (i.e., equipment specially designed to withstand the rigors of military operations and combat).

Certain offices in the Department of Defense use CD-ROM for internal use to prevent unauthorized access and/or tampering that could occur with computers. Instead of selecting CD-ROM as the medium of choice for information, most military applications use WORM optical disk technology which permits the storage of images of engineering drawings and maintenance of complete files of all documentation revisions and updates, and allows equipment operators to annotate their manuals. It is expected that the DoD will use both CD-ROM and WORM, often in hybrid information systems.

Advanced Systems Development, Inc. (ASD) has recently designed a dual CD-ROM unit specifically for U.S. government users under a contract to provide CD-ROM storage capabilities to DoD. The firm has integrated two Hitachi CD-ROM half-height drives in a specially designed casing for proper ventilation and multi-voltage power supply for international usage. The unit controls 2.6 gigabytes with a single controller board. This storage system will allow manipulation of an industrial database being processed by ASD and Reference Technology, Inc. ASD's objective is to increase personnel productivity for those who use this database at almost 30,000 government sites.

While NASA uses WORM technology mainly to distribute satellite data, its Jet Propulsion Laboratory has selected CD-ROM for storing space images on earth. Satellites transmit the data from the space exploration missions, such as Voyager's fly-by of the moons of Jupiter and Uranus, for storage on magnetic tape. Researchers all over the world have access to these tapes. However, since one mission can generate 250 tapes, retrieving the data and maintaining the tapes can present problems that optical storage can solve. NASA has also selected CD-ROM systems for storing technical manuals for the planned orbiting space station.

Regulations

Relying on paper indices sometimes proves unsuccessful due to such limitations as the use of only major terms or their principal occurrences or changing terminology over a period of time. Full-text searching may solve these problems, but it may also produce a larger number of "hits" to examine. CD-ROM technology permits users to combine occurrences of terms and search full-text to obtain random access to particular regulations without concern for increasing telecommunications costs. Anybody working with government regulations such as lawyers, legislators, judges, lobbyists, contractors, etc., should find this a valuable tool.

ALDE Publishing has developed several products that provide full-text access to selected government publications. Its Federal Acquisition/Procurement Disc (Title 41/48) covers Title 41/48 dealing with U.S. government acquisition and procurement issues. The Title 20 USC/CFR disc covers Title 20, Social Security. Title 26 USC/CFR deals with Title 26, Internal Revenue code and regulations while Title 42 USC/CFR covers the Public Health Code and Health and Human Services Regulations. All of these databases include material from the *U.S. Code* and the *Code of Federal Regulations,* thus speeding access to material that previously required much research.

The company also publishes USSR Source 21, a Soviet reference library containing 30 megabytes of Soviet-designed software, the complete *Communist Manifesto,* gross economic indicators since 1960, descriptions of space launches and payloads, technical information on weapons systems since 1965, USSR almanac/world records, cartographic information, transcripts of Academy of Science annual meetings, *Pravda, Izvestia, TASS,* organizational charts of agencies such as the KGB, and biographies of Politburo members since 1912. ALDE plans to publish other foreign national databases that will contain material gathered from public domain data collections available from sources in the United States and the other country as well as from publishers with specific information on that country that are willing to work with ALDE on a royalty basis.

VLS, Inc. markets a CD-ROM version of the *Code of Federal Regulations* under the name OPTEXT which includes the complete Code, Titles 1-50, and aims to provide the capability of replacing the print version. The product identification scheme is a little confusing, partly due to the eccentric manner in which the GPO releases the data. VLS provides a unique service, OPTEXT Online Demo, which allows dial-up access to use and evaluate the CD-ROM database.

TMS, Inc. has three titles of the *Code of Federal Regulations* on CD-ROM discs. The company uses them to demonstrate how TMS search software handles large full-text databases such as the Internal Revenue Code, the Social Security Database, and the Public Health Code. Although TMS, a data-preparation and search-software firm, has no plans to market the discs, it is interested in attracting clients that want to sell the entire code on CD-ROM.

Another CD-ROM disc developed by Environmental Resources Management (ERM) Computer Services, Inc., ENFLEX INFO, provides an updated compilation of the full-text of all federal and state environmental regulations. ERM staff organize and index the information to meet compliance, monitoring, permits, and reporting requirements. The Nuclear Regulatory Commission is working on a Nuclear Waste Management Document Management System to contain the full-text of

Figure 19. CD-ROM Databases Available from
Private Industry and Their Counterparts

Private Industry	Government Agency
BiblioFile	Library of Congress
Cat CD450	
LaserQuest	MARC
M/100 with DisCon	MARC-S
PC/MARC	CDMARC Subjects
	CDMARC Names
GPO on SilverPlatter	Government Printing Office
Monthly Catalog	
LePac: Government Documents	Monthly Catalog (paper)
Option	
Small Business Consultant	
StatPack	
BiblioMed	National Library of Medicine
BRS/Colleague Disc	
Compact Cambridge	MEDLINE (online, CD-ROM)
MEDLINE (Dialog, OCLC,	
SilverPlatter	
Medline Knowledge Finder	
AGRICOLA (Dialog, OCLC	National Agricultural Library
SilverPlatter)	AGRICOLA (online, CD-ROM)
NTIS (Dialog, OCLC	NTIS
SilverPlatter)	NTIS (online, CD-ROM)
CD/Biotech	
Chembank	
NATASHA	
OSH-ROM	
CD/Corporate	
Compact Disclosure	
One Source	Postal Service
AVS+	
Bookshelf	National Postal Services
Flash+4	Directory (paper)
ZIP+4	
1929-1986 Business Indicators	Bureau of the Census
Census of Agriculture	Census Test Disc #1
County Statistics	Census Test Disc #2
Building Sciences Information	
Engineering Information	
Material Safety Data Sheets	
Material Safety Data System	
Parts Master	
Personnet	
Technical Logistics Reference	
Network	
GEOdisc	U.S. Geological Survey
Hydrodata	
MUNDOCART/CD	Event CD
Supermap	
Enflex Info	U.S. Code (paper, microfiche)
Federal Acquisition/Procurement	Code of Federal Regulations
Disc	(paper microfiche)
OPTEXT	
Title 20 USC/CFR	
Title 26 USC/CFR	
Title 42 USC/CFR	
TMS Research	

all documents related to nuclear waste disposal site licensing actions.

The Federal Deposit Insurance Corporation (FDIC) is working on a CD-ROM disc that will contain the FDIC Rules and Regulations, all examiners reference manuals, and legal text to complement or replace its existing looseleaf service. Information Handling Services has developed a prototype disc of Comptroller General Decisions and Equal Employment Opportunity Commission Decisions that includes 13,000 pronouncements.

Summary

While many government agencies use commercially available CD-ROM discs and a few are developing their own applications, there seems to be a level of caution in the adoption process. Aside from the costs of the microcomputers, the prices of CD-ROM drives and most of the disc products remain relatively high. These costs escalate even more to produce a disc that may have limited distribution and return on investment.

Many information professionals argue for the concept of "human-readability" that guarantees that the information remain in a usable form over the long term. Concern is expressed about the future availability of equipment to read the data currently being recorded because it relies on computer/optical information systems as an intermediary between the user and the data which no longer appear in human-readable form.

On the other hand, optical media seem to offer solutions to paper storage and the associated filing and maintenance problems, the need for quick record retrieval, the desire to transport documents rapidly with no deterioration in quality, and the need to preserve original records, many of which remain in damaged or poor condition.

The National Academy of Sciences recommends the use of paper or microfilm for archival purposes over optical and magnetic media.[3] It cites the following as its principal reasons:

• permanence (of the discs and the technologies)
• standardization
• cost effectiveness

The Academy claims that paper and microfilm, when properly made and cared for, may last hundreds of years. Magnetic disks and tape, on the other hand, last only 10 to 20 years while optical disks have an unknown lifetime. Some estimates put it at 20 years or less; others place it at 50 years or more.

Rapid changes in the optical industry appear as a deterrent to early adoption since hardware and software now available to read optical disks may not be available in the future. The study committee identified seven or eight very complete changes in magnetic tape format over the last 30 years. As software continues to undergo revision, the user needs to convert any machine-readable data periodically for use with new systems. Organizations that have permanent information, low-level use, and no need to change or update would not find data conversion cost-beneficial. Equipment obsolescence could become a serious problem in such an environment.

CD-ROM technology promises a more convenient medium of information distribution, but the relatively small base of installed equipment deters some government agencies from adopting it. The information-poor who could benefit most from CD-ROM are often the technology-poor who cannot take advantage of the medium's power. The relatively high costs of most products make them prohibitive to the economically poor. Yet entrepreneurs and information vendors have found—and continue to find—new opportunities to develop successful products.

More than half of the U.S. gross national product comes from service industries, most of which rely heavily on information, and for them CD-ROM offers a competitive edge, especially coupled with on-line searching, for quick access to large quantities of data. Although the government collects and produces immense amounts of information, it wants to divest itself from any "non-governmental" functions such as the sale or distribution of this information—regardless of the format. Rather it seems content with letting the private sector develop and add value to its products and find new opportunities to make a profit.

On the other hand, the government wants to protect automated data systems and telecommunications against unauthorized access. While this may limit the free exchange of scientific information and lead to censorship, the purpose is to control foreign access to U.S. information for reasons of national security. Ironically, much of the U.S. private information industry—including CD-ROM producers—is now foreign-owned. This includes online vendors such as BRS, ORBIT, INFOLINE, DIALCOM, DATA STAR, and ESA; services such as Congressional Information Service, INSPEC, METADEX, Derwent, Predicasts, and Excerpta Medica; and publishers such as Bowker, Warren Gorham Lamont, Clark Boardman, Van Nostrand Reinhold, Medical Economics, Greenwood Press, Aspen Systems, Gale Research Company, Capital Services, Information Handling Services, Doubleday, New American Library, E.P. Dutton, Henry Holt, Viking, Literary Guild, Bantam, and Dell—which represent 15 percent of U.S. book sales and some major players in CD-ROM publishing.

Law

The legal profession (i.e., practicing attorneys) often projects an image of conservatism which can demonstrate itself in a reluctance to embrace new technologies. Part of this is due to a low awareness level. Lawyers, as a group, demonstrate the same attitudes toward automation as the average consumer. Many have computer phobia and a reluctance to climb the learning curve or to pay their staff to do so when they have little or no assurance that invested time and expense will pay off. Attorneys have accepted word processing much later than other professional groups.

Another factor affecting the legal profession's attitude toward CD-ROM technology may be the billing practices common in the profession. Legal researchers frequently use pass-through billing to charge their clients directly for their time, services, and online searches. The fixed cost of optical systems makes this practice seem impossible, and could raise the overhead for users of such systems. Even though automation permits increased volume of work, this does not necessarily translate into increased profit.

Most lawyers do not perceive CD-ROM as providing sufficient cost savings over traditional sources to justify a change. Paper and microform, supplemented by online searching, provide adequate access to the material. The profession is so familiar with its work that it usually finds it easier to maintain the *status quo* than to introduce changes that may disrupt things.

While practicing attorneys may demonstrate a reluctance to accept new technologies, law libraries do not appear much different from their academic counterparts in accepting CD-ROM. They view part of their service as educating their clientele to new sources of information and searching procedures. In fact, adoption in law libraries may eventually influence adoption in legal agencies.

Because the practice of law encompasses many different areas, such as real estate and property law, tax law, corporate law, and criminal law, some firms may find it useful to subscribe to CD-ROM products targeted at specific vertical markets such as business, medicine, and education. Attorneys who focus their work on specific markets probably present a better marketing opportunity for CD-ROM than the "general practitioner." Products aimed at vertical markets may target both practitioners and attorneys who work in those areas.

Bibliography

As a parallel to the library CD-ROM market, the first products to appear in the legal area were subsets of the MARC bibliographic databases, such as UTLAS's LAWMARC, to facilitate identifying and cataloging legal materials. Information Access Company's LegalTrac, an add-on to its videodisc-based InfoTrac system, provided the first index to legal materials in optical format. But, unlike InfoTrac, it did not migrate to CD-ROM until mid-1988 when IAC switched to CD-ROM as the primary optical storage medium. The firm expects this change to result in a savings of up to 30 percent for subscribers. More recently H.W. Wilson introduced a CD-ROM version of its *Index to Legal Periodicals* as part of its WILSONDISC family. While both products resemble their print counterparts in terms of content, they increase access to citations, sometimes by providing additional access points. LegalTrac limits the search keys to author name or subject while the Index to Legal Periodicals uses author, title, and subject search keys and accommodates Boolean logic to narrow the results.

Full-Text Searching

While these products facilitate the work of law librarians, practicing attorneys require better access to the text of various laws and court decisions that represent an extensive volume of material. It is easy to get lost in the maze of references or to overlook significant, but obscure pronouncements. Lawyers need to be able to locate cases by keyword or elements that can link one case to another. They also need to examine summary material or interpretations. This has spurred some companies to concentrate on full-text search and retrieval of the legal documents themselves.

Wang Laboratories, Inc., West Publishing Co., and Reference Technology, Inc. (RTI) announced, at the Third International Conference on CD-ROM (March 1988) sponsored by Microsoft, a cooperative effort to provide CD-ROM products and services for the legal community. West's giant full-text WESTLAW database (along with Mead Data Central's LEXIS) has become one of the legal researcher's standard sources of online information. West can master part or all of the WESTLAW database onto one or more CD-ROM discs. It has also developed publishing software that formats data for CD-ROM discs. This software allows complete customization of information, including plural and synonym word indexing and publisher-defined hypertext. Wang, which has a large market share of the installed base of equipment currently installed in law offices, is developing end-user research software to access and retrieve information from the discs produced using West Publishing's software.

Both companies have licensed their software to Reference Technology, Inc. for sublicensing to its customers who will be able to access update information through West's online system using the Wang research software. These software and system products conform to the High Sierra/ISO CD-ROM standards and use the Microsoft CD-ROM Extensions to ensure compatibility between the CD-ROM discs and drives.

Mead Data Central produces and maintains the LEXIS database. LEXIS, together with West Publishing Company's WESTLAW, accounts for virtually all the machine-readable databases that legal researchers use either directly or indirectly through gateways. The firm is conducting focus groups and market tests that will probably result in several CD-ROM products for the legal and accounting markets. Its purchase several years ago of Micromedex, Inc., a producer of several pharmaceutical indices on CD-ROM, is expected to facilitate the development of CD-ROM products for this market. Mead may face a difficult challenge trying to enter this field alone with a CD-ROM product and it is certain to face formidable competition from the West, Wang, RTI alliance.

The Michie Company has produced a CD-ROM version of the Code of the Commonwealth of Virginia, the only state code in this format at present. While Hawaii is the only state that does not have its laws on an online service, it does have them in machine-readable form at a large electronic publishing concern in California. The Michie Company is considering storing this information on CD-ROM.

Tax Law

While government regulations on CD-ROM (discussed in the previous section) may interest some attorneys, tax laws concern everyone, especially tax lawyers, accountants, and businesses. Because of this, CD-ROM applications involving this material may constitute a successful product in this area and offer the means for CD-ROM to enter the profession.

Prentice-Hall, Inc. leads this field with the PHINet tax resource library. PHINet contains regulations, cases, rulings, letter rulings, and administrative interpretations that make up the critical body of tax law. Since Reference Technology, Inc. mastered this disc as well as those of other competitors such as Tax Analysts, some measure of disc interchangeability is ensured.

Besides the PHINet tax resource library, tax lawyers and accountants currently have CD-ROM access to nearly one gigabyte of primary tax material that includes code, legislative histories, private letter rulings, and court decisions. The main source material for The Tax Library (Tax Analysts) is made up of seven discs. An eighth disc provides quarterly updates to the collection with access to the online service for more recent information.

The Internal Revenue Service (IRS), which spends close to $1 million per year for research on LEXIS, is evaluating CD-ROM technology as a means to decrease search costs and increase personnel productivity. It is considering storing both the Internal Revenue Code and the IRS Tax Revenue Rulings and Procedures on disc.

Here again, we find RTI working with Tax Analysts, publishers of *Tax Notes Today* in print and electronic form, to develop a CD-ROM version as part of a proposal to the Internal Revenue Service. RTI has also begun a pilot project to master and produce "Tax Court Opinions" from 1982 to the present.

Online Computer Systems, Inc. has stored Tax Forms on Demand, a package of federal and state income tax forms, on CD-ROM. This disc inaugurates a series of demand publishing products the firm is developing. Every agency that has provided tax forms to the public can attest to the headaches they cause in trying to maintain an orderly and adequate supply of forms and publications and the resulting abuse their staff have to endure when the supply has been depleted. Tax Forms on Demand should eliminate these problems by always having the documents available for personal copying.

Other Legal-Related Vertical Markets

Information providers have also identified other vertical markets or niches in those markets that have opened some new horizons for their CD-ROM products. In so doing, they must beware not to over-specialize. Information providers need to have a broad enough base to allow them to recuperate the costs of their investment or to find a clientele willing and able to pay more than its fair share to enjoy the advantages of CD-ROM.

Quantum Access, Inc. compiles state and federal regulations on CD-ROM for specific vertical markets such as education and the oil and gas industries. Its first product, the State Education Encyclopedia, contains all the legislative and regulatory material that a Texas school administrator might need: state legislation, policies and procedures of the Texas Education Agency, curriculum guides, transcripts of administrative hearings, court cases, and state interpretations of administrative hearings. Previously, this information was available only by searching through the Texas Education Agency archives.

The firm's second offering, the Texas Attorney General Documents, contains the full-text of the documents from the Texas Attorney General's Office from 1979 to 1986. This CD-ROM disc also includes the Open Records Act Decisions, letter advisories, and constitutional convention advisories.

Summary

One obstacle to more widespread use of CD-ROM databases in the legal area may result from the nature of legal publication. Many materials come in looseleaf format on a weekly or monthly basis—an expensive undertaking to keep current on disc.

Another obstacle seems to hinge on the disc's storage capacity and the availability of seamless interfaces to the online services. A single CD-ROM can store only a small amount of the information available through the large WESTLAW and LEXIS databases that are used regularly by legal researchers. While producers can master subsets of the database on a CD-ROM disc along with software to continue the search online for more comprehensive or more current information, many seem reluctant to do so because of the uncertainty of this market.

One legal information provider, H.W. Wilson, has published its Index to Legal Periodicals on CD-ROM which provides unlimited access to the same database on Wilsonline as part of its subscription fee. This has had a positive impact on product acceptance because the information user can now get thorough coverage of a topic at a fixed cost. CD-ROM technology may appear to decrease costs through the elimination of the need to house large quantities of materials in hard copy or through the reduction in online searching costs. While these may represent significant savings with office space valued at $25 to $30 per square foot and online search costs averaging around $120 per hour, any potential saving may disappear when the high cost of CD-ROM database subscriptions are taken into consideration. Small legal firms may find it difficult to justify such a purchase.

In addition, there is the problem of pass-through billing which conflicts with the fixed cost of CD-ROM systems. "To overcome this disadvantage, at least one laser disc system has built in a program that gives a cost for each search conducted. Such built-in billing programs may help users determine and recoup their individual search costs and, with heavily used databases, even make a profit from laser disc systems."[4]

Conclusion

SilverPlatter has the greatest number of CD-ROM products on the market (mostly from government-sponsored sources) while Reference Technology, Inc. seems to be the vendor of choice for producing many of the databases for some government agencies and for the legal profession (such as the Customs Department, the IRS, and its collaboration with Wang Laboratories and West Publishing Co. as well as work on PHINet and The Tax Library). The predominance of these two companies in these areas should facilitate the interchangeability of discs among applications that use other products from these agencies.

While the High Sierra volume and file structure format and Microsoft's CD-ROM Extensions go a long way in bringing about some standardization and compatibility, many applications still do not use one or both of these features. Some vendors that follow the High Sierra standards but do not use Microsoft's CD-ROM Extensions state that the device drivers the CD-ROM Extensions use do not maximize the performance of their products. While there may be good reason to select non-standard products, users should do so knowingly, fully conscious that until every product uses the same device drivers compatibility problems will persist.

Meanwhile, Microsoft continues to improve its CD-ROM Extensions. We can expect a gradual evolution and eventual migration of most—if not all—CD-ROM products to operate in this environment. The use of common device drivers will make changing discs as easy as switching from a word processor to a spreadsheet program with only the added step of exchanging the disc in the CD-ROM drive.

While some products already have interfaces with other software packages such as word processors and spreadsheets, more frequent use of these features for exporting data for manipulation and for insertion of user-specific data can be expected. Also, further refinement and use of hypertext that will allow users to link data and concepts to facilitate exploration of new avenues in information is forthcoming.

Among other things, the use of artificial intelligence software will eventually include the ability to process information using natural language, thereby eliminating the need to master several different search languages and protocols. For example, users will be able to search the *U.S. Code* or the *Code of Federal Regulations* using the same terms regardless of whether they have ALDE Publishing Co.'s product or that of VLS. This would also apply to the many versions of MEDLINE and other databases. (See Chapter 2 for a comparison of the software of eight different CD-ROM MEDLINE products.)

First-generation CD-ROM discs contained single databases from a single source. Second-generation discs are combining multiple databases from one or more sources such as census data and state maps. Some products are integrating the data so the user can search everything as a unit (e.g., Chem-bank and CD/Corporate). Both first- and second-generation products have relied on machine-readable data. Third-generation discs will probably contain material currently in traditional formats converted to digital form by means of optical scanning. Because of the high costs involved in such conversions, these applications will be driven by market demand. Vendors will respond to such requests only if the market can support the conversion costs.

While applications for the government and legal areas may neglect to use CD-ROM's audio capabilities, future products can be expected to make increasing use of its graphic capabilities. In addition to the familiar charts and graphs, motion and still-frame graphics such as animation and photos will be stored on CD-ROM. The U.S. Department of Customs project that Reference Technology, Inc. is working on may use this feature.

Enhancing geographic or satellite data with graphics on CD-ROM could provide realistic images that could serve in training pilots. Astronauts could familiarize themselves with the terrain of distant planets and anticipate any navigational problems without risking their lives. Companies involved in prospecting and exploration could also rely on such applications to perform computer simulation or modeling and thereby make better decisions.

Notes

1. Desmarais, Norman. "CD-ROMs Proliferate." *Optical Information Systems* 9:1 (forthcoming from Meckler Corporation) and *The Librarian's CD-ROM Handbook.* Westport, CT: Meckler Corporation, 1988.
2. Peverett, Tracy. "Will CD-ROM Shine in the DP World?" *Canadian Datasystems* 19 (10): 55.
3. *Preservation of Historical Records—The National Archives & Records Administration Study of Preservation Media.* Washington, D.C.: National Academy of Sciences.
4. Kauffman, S. Blair. "Laser Disc Applications for Law Libraries." *CD-ROM Librarian* 3:1 (January 1988): 17.

Appendix A: Directory of CD-ROM Government and Law Applications

ALDE Publishing (Applied Laser Disc Efficiencies)
7840 Computer Avenue
P.O. Box 35326
Minneapolis, MN 55435
612-835-5240

BRS Information Technologies
1200 Route 7
Latham, NY 12110
800-468-0908
215-254-0233

Cambridge Scientific Abstracts
5161 River Road
Bethesda, MD 20816
301-951-1400

Chadwyck-Healey Inc.
1101 King Street
Alexandria, VA 22314
703-683-4890

DIALOG Information Services Inc.
3460 Hillview Avenue
Palo Alto, CA 94304
800-3-DIALOG
415-858-2700

Digital Diagnostics Inc.
601 University Avenue
Suite 255
Sacramento, CA 95825
916-781-1196

Environmental Resources Management, Computer Serv.
999 West Chester Pike
West Chester PA 19382
800-544-3118

Faxon Company, The
15 Southwest Park
Westwood, MA 02090
800-225-6055
617-329-3350 x 465

General Research Corporation, Library Systems
5383 Hollister Avenue
Santa Barbara CA 93111
800-235-6788
805-964-7724

Geovision, Inc.
270 Scientific Drive
Suite 1
Norcross, GA 30092
404-448-8224

H.W. Wilson Company
950 University Avenue
Bronx, NY 10452
212-588-8400

Information Access Company
357 Lakeside Drive
Foster City CA 94404
800-227-8431
415-591-2333

Information Design Inc.
P.O. Box 7130
1300 Charleston Road
Mountain View, CA 94039-7130
415-969-7990

Innovative Technology, Inc.
2927 Jones Branch Drive
McLean, VA 22102
703-734-3000

International Association for Scientific Computing
1030 East Duane Avenue
Suite E
Sunnyvale, CA 94086
408-730-9616

Knowledge Access International
2685 Marine Way
Suite 1305
Mountain View, CA 94043
415-969-0606

Library Corporation, The
P.O. Box 40035
Washington, D.C. 20016
800-624-0559
304-725-7220

Library of Congress Cataloging Distribution Service
Customer Services Section
Washington, D.C. 20541
202-287-6171

Library Systems and Services, Inc.
20251 Century Boulevard
Germantown, MD 20874-1162
800-638-8725
301-428-3400

Lotus Development Corporation
55 Cambridge Parkway
Cambridge, MA 02142
800-521-6667
617-938-6667

Mead Data Central
9393 Springboro Pike
P.O. Box 933
Dayton, OH 45401
513-865-6889

Michie Company, The
P.O. Box 7587
Charlottesville, VA 22906
804-295-6171

Microsoft Corporation
16011 N.E. 36th Way
Box 97017
Redmond, WA 98073-9717
206-882-8080

NASA-Johnson Space Center
2101 NASA Road
Bldg. 1 #660
Houston, TX 77058
713-483-0123

National Institute of Building Sciences
1015 15th Street N.W.
Suite 700
Washington, D.C. 20005
202-347-5710

National Library of Medicine
National Institute of Health
8600 Rockville Pike

Bethesda, MD 20894
301-496-6308

National Safety Data Corporation
259 West Road
Salem, CT 06415
203-859-1162

National Standards Association, Inc.
5161 River Road
Bethesda, MD 20816
800-638-8094
301-951-1389

National Technical Information Service (NTIS)
5285 Port Royal Road
Springfield, VA 22161
703-487-4805

OCLC
6565 Frantz Road
Dublin, OH 43017-0702
614-764-6000

Omni Computer Systems, Inc.
670 Centre Street
Jamaica Plain, MA 02130
617-522-4760

Online Computer Systems, Inc.
20251 Century Boulevard
Germantown, MD 20874
800-922-9204
301-428-3700

PHINet (Prentice Hall Information Network)
1 Gulf & Western Plaza
New York, NY 10023
212-373-8600

Quantum Access Inc.
1700 West Loop South
Suite 1460
Houston TX 77027

800-822-4211
713-622-3211

Reference Technology, Inc.
5655 Lindero Canyon Road
Building 100
Westlake Village, CA 91362
818-991-1202

SilverPlatter Information, Inc.
37 Walnut Street
Wellesley Hills, MA 02181
617-239-0306

Slater Hall Information Products
1522 K Street N.W.
Suite 522
Washington, D.C. 20005
202-682-1350

Tax Analysts
6830 N. Fairfax Drive
Arlington, VA 22213
800-336-0439
703-532-1850

TMS, Inc.
110 West Third Street
P.O. Box 1358
Stillwater, OK 74076
405-377-0880

U.S. Bureau of Census
Data Users Service Division
Washington, D.C. 20233
202-763-4100

U.S. Dept. of Agriculture SEA/TIS
National Agricultural Library Building
Room 300
Beltsville, MD 20705
301-344-3829

U.S. Geological Survey
804 National Center
Reston VA 22092
703-648-4000

U.S. West Knowledge Engineering
4380 South Syracuse Street
Suite 600
Denver, CO 80237
800-222-0920
303-694-4200

Utlas International
2150 Shattuck Avenue
Suite 402
Berkeley, CA 94704
415-841-9442

VLS, Inc. (Video Laser Systems)
310 S. Reynolds Road
Toledo, OH 43615
419-536-5820

Wang Laboratories, Inc.
1 Industrial Avenue
Lowell, MA 01851
800-22LINCS
617-459-5000

West Publishing Co.
P.O. Box 64526
St. Paul, MN 55164
612-228-2738

4

CD-ROM in General Education

SANDRA KAY HELSEL

General education, kindergarten through graduate school, was largely unaware of CD-ROM hardware and courseware at the beginning
of 1988. When a leading researcher in reading and teacher education
asked "What is CD-ROM?" she reflected general education's collective
nescience regarding CD-ROM technology (Dole, 1988). Most educators
who teach in the thousands of elementary, secondary, and university
classrooms in the United States have had minimal or no exposure to
CD-ROM as an educational medium to date. Eventually, it will be this
very group of teachers and teacher-educators who will determine
whether CD-ROM technology will realize its potential in education—just
as this group and its earlier counterparts have determined education's
acceptance or rejection of earlier technologies.

It is difficult (but not impossible) for educators to either observe
CD-ROM in educational settings or read about CD-ROM in the educational and popular press. The amount of information available to the
general education community concerning CD-ROM continues to be almost as limited as the actual educational usage of CD-ROM. Few educators know that in March 1988 Apple Computer introduced a CD-ROM
drive that will be compatible with education's favorite Apple II computer series (Macon, 1988). Also, few educators have access to CD-
ROM programs that are directly applicable to students, administrators,
or students.

One of the first CD-ROM programs directed at students is the K-8
comprehensive curriculum developed by Education Systems Corporation (ECS) in San Diego. Although ECS reported that 300 schools
were using its curriculum by spring 1988 (Scanlon, 1988), that number
represents only .3 percent of the total school sites registered in the
1987 Federal *Digest of Education Statistics*. For administrative applications, Texas is the only state to have its "State Educational Encyclopedia" published on CD-ROM (by Quantum Access). And for teachers,
"Science Helper" marketed by PC-SIG, Inc., seems to be the only
CD-ROM-based "teacher resource center" yet available. This disc

contains 918 lesson plans that teachers can access as a resource when teaching traditional science themes in grades K-8.

As for written information about CD-ROM in the educational press, there were no listings for CD of any kind in education's *CIJE: Current Index to Journals in Education* as late as February 1988. Neither were there references to CD technology on ERIC, the educational database (even though ERIC was being marketed then on disc by SilverPlatter and DIALOG). Any individual interested in reading about CD-ROM in the educational press would have had to scan individual journals article-by-article and page-by-page for mention of the technology. Using that laborious method, a diligent researcher would have found references to CD-ROM interspersed randomly throughout articles in educational publications specifically dedicated to instructional technology.

It is only natural that instructional technologists have been the first to acknowledge and endorse CD-ROM as an educational medium. That same group also endorsed interactive videodisc (IVD) early in the 1980s; its specialized publications enthusiastically described IVD two to three years before general education knew videodisc existed.

Education has a small (but well-informed and articulate) subgroup of technologists with whom the CD-ROM industry has already been or soon will be acquainted. Education's technology proponents attend the various electronic conferences en masse and discuss the various computer-driven technologies with great understanding and sophistication. It would be easy for any computer-related industry to overestimate the influence of education's technological subculture. What may not be so apparent to those outside formal education is that any number of subcultures flourish (and often clash) within the U.S. educational community. For example, educational researchers are often squared off against self-proclaimed "practitioners," while teachers and administrators exhibit extreme differences in their respective approaches to education (Chilcott, 1983). Representatives of electronic media firms most likely meet and interact with individuals from education's technology-oriented subgroup whose members have been called "technocrats" by educational anthropologist Wolcott (1977).

However, it is the basic premise of this chapter that it will not be the educational technocrats who will ultimately determine the education market's acceptance and usage of CD-ROM. Technocrats have had remarkably little influence over the mass integration of computers into the K-12 school system during this decade. Even more recently (mid-1980s), technocrats misread the future of IVD in the classroom and were still busy writing of individual videodisc learning stations when school teachers had already developed their own usage pattern and had started using videodisc machines as a source of high-quality illustrations for traditional lectures. The forebears of today's technocrat contingent also failed to influence the integration of earlier technologies such as radio or television into yesterday's classrooms.

Instead, it will be general education—with its traditional classroom structure and its thousands of elementary and secondary classroom teachers as well as its university-based teacher education system—that will eventually determine the success of CD-ROM as an educational medium. CD-ROM's educational potential will be realized only when teachers routinely plan and include the technology in everyday classroom activities—and the classroom has traditionally defined the terms on which new technologies have been adopted. Therefore, the educational market's acceptance of CD-ROM will be championed *if* the technology can be aligned with general education as it functions today.

This chapter discusses CD-ROM technology in terms of its possible alignment with the pivotal elements of the two separate but interrelated institutions that control formal education in the United States: (1) the public schools (K-12); and (2) the university-based teacher training departments. The critical factors within the public educational institution include ideology, economics, social actors (e.g., teachers, administrators, and students), as well as education's place in the larger sociopolitical environment. The relationship of CD-ROM technology to each of these elements is discussed throughout this chapter. Recommendations are also offered concerning future CD-ROM courseware that will make use of the technology's unique ability to meet the educational needs of the 1990s.

CD-ROM and the Traditional Classroom Configuration

First it is necessary to examine the notion that CD-ROM would be better served by working within the existing and fundamentally conservative educational system than by planning for its implementation into a revolutionary technology-driven school often forecast for the future. Education has a long history of surviving unchanged against well-planned and well-intentioned efforts to shift its approaches from something other than the traditional teacher-centered classroom with 30 students. Rhetoric predicting a technological restructuring of the public schools often surfaces in research articles or at computer conferences, but that rhetoric is simply not being translated into action at the local level or in the teacher training colleges. The traditional classroom with its autonomous teacher is the paradigm with which CD-ROM hardware and software vendors will realistically have to work for at least the next 10 years. There are no indications that the educational process will become either student-driven or technology-centered as opposed to its present teacher-centered orientation.

Instead, it is almost certain that we will leave the teacher in place, eventually supported and supplemented by technology. CD-ROM hardware and software producers need to develop their products in harmony with the needs of an autonomous teacher facing a self-contained classroom, and in tune with the needs of the students of the 1990s—whose numbers will increasingly be from today's minority groups and poor families, and thus may be increasingly diagnosed with physical and emotional handicaps (Hodgkinson, 1988). The exact nature of CD-ROM programs that conform to the traditional classroom and meet student learning needs of the 1990s will be discussed at length later in this chapter. But several key issues regarding the continuation of the self-contained classroom must be emphasized at this point.

The belief that the traditional classroom will continue without complete technological restructuring in America's schools is based upon two observations. The first is that the powerful and influential leaders of our current "second wave of school reform" movement are calling for what is consolidation and strengthening of the traditional classroom teacher's role. That movement is advocating that teachers be given a more active voice in what to teach and how to teach it as opposed to the somewhat limited authority they have been given until this point.

For example, reform spokesman Ernest Boyer (1987) urges teachers to control education in the classroom. The influential Carnegie Forum Task Force on Teaching as a Profession recommends that teachers be given greater discretion and autonomy (1986). The editor of education's powerful *Phi Delta Kappan* has asserted that "teacher empowerment" is the key to an effective school (Gough, 1988). According to the current thinking among school reformers, teachers will perform their tasks with the necessary assurance and authority if they are given access to decision making. It hardly seems likely that a newly enfranchised teaching force will surrender the classroom to technology. Ideally, however, such a teaching force will use its decision-making powers in such a way that educational technology (in this case CD-ROM) will be integrated meaningfully into the traditional classroom structure.

The second observation concerning the continuation of the traditional classroom is drawn from educational history. A clear historical pattern has been established concerning what happens when new technologies enter the schoolhouse door. Simply stated, teachers tailor technology to the dimensions of traditional practice; those technologies that could not be tailored to the traditional educational system have been rejected or modified. Each technology that has been adopted by the public school system in this century was integrated into the classroom in such a manner that the traditional classroom environment has remained unaltered.

These two factors have direct consequences for the public school's adoption of CD-ROM technology. One of the prime tenets of the "teacher empowerment" movement is that teachers must be made more knowledgeable about subject matter and pedagogy as well as the application of new resources within the traditional classroom structure. CD-ROM technology is poised for entry into schools at a time when teachers are being urged to become knowledgeable about the appropriate use of such resources as technologies (Lieberman, 1988). This is a prime opportunity for CD-ROM producers and developers to work with and for the ongoing dynamics of education.

Teacher inservice is highly recommended as a vehicle for school improvement by second-wave reformers and teacher empowerment advocates (Maerof, 1988). With proper planning, the inservice format could become beneficial as a vehicle with which to increase practicing teachers' knowledge of CD-ROM. The design and implementation of qualitative inservice for practicing teachers will certainly become more common as the second-wave reform movement grows. CD-ROM firms may well be advised to offer districts staff and financial resources to support the technological components of the inservices, at least initially. A system known as "train the trainers" could be instituted for the future—teachers introduced to CD-ROM technology at the initial inservices can later serve as in-district trainers and resource persons.

Furthermore, the second-wave reformers have acknowledged the inadequacy of past efforts to acquaint teachers with learning technologies as well as the use of those technologies. For example, a report to the Ford Foundation from the Urban Mathematics Collaborative has pointed out that most of today's teachers do not know how to apply new ideas or resources within the traditional classroom structure. According to the report, "For too long, materials have simply been given to teachers...most teachers are unaware of how to ask for and use external resouces" (Romberg and Pittman, 1985, p. 15). Relatedly, an extensive amount of highly specific information describing various teacher training programs for computers is now available. For example, veterans of education's computer revolution found that it was best not to tell teachers about the use of computers, but to train teachers *with* the use of computers. Any future training programs developed especially for CD-ROM should benefit from today's critical assessment of earlier teacher training methodologies.

Introduction of New Technologies

Classrooms exhibited a remarkable stability when the new technologies of this century were introduced into education. Teachers have a "persistent core of practices" that are extremely resilient and efficient

(Cuban, 1986). Today, as in the past, the teacher lectures and questions while the student listens and answers; the teacher assigns passages in texts and the student reads the assigned material. Historically, new technologies have either conformed to the classroom teacher's "persistent core of practices" or have been rejected. Education has sometimes created interesting and unforeseen modifications in the usage patterns of technology, but those modifications always caused the technology to conform to the traditional classroom paradigm.

For all its technological capabilities, CD-ROM has no characteristics that are powerful enough to override these "persistent core of practices." Technologies have always evolved in unanticipated directions and it is possible that CD-ROM evolution will lead to learning courseware not yet foreseeable. But for the most part, CD-ROM's integration into education will have many parallels to earlier technologies, such as the microcomputer and IVD. Therefore, a review of several of the technologies that entered the classroom in the twentieth century and their acceptance (always in a modified form) or their rejection offers valuable insights into what could happen to CD-ROM in the public schools.

Each new technology has been welcomed with an initial enthusiasm that predicted extraordinary changes in teacher practice and student learning. In 1922, Thomas Edison wrote, "I believe that the motion picture is destined to revolutionize our educational system and that in a few years it will supplant largely, if not entirely, the use of textbooks." That same kind of enthusiasm has greeted each technology in turn, from the motion picture, to radio, to television and, more recently, to computers. In fact, Stanley Pogrow (1982) warned education that it would face an "environmental collapse" unless it adopted computers wholesale. But despite the initial furor and enthusiasm over each new technology, the classroom has essentially remained the same and it will probably continue to remain as is even after CD-ROM has been adopted in the classroom. Certainly, Edison's predictions about the motion picture supplanting textbooks were never realized—teachers occasionally schedule and show movies as a supplement to the regular curriculum.

Radio. Radio is a technology that briefly courted the public schools of America in the 1930s and 1940s but was eventually rejected. The data on how many classrooms tuned into the so-called "textbooks of the air" are fragmentary, but Larry Cuban (1985) claims that the amount of time spent listening to radio in classrooms was infinitesimal. It wasn't that radios weren't available, for surveys taken in 1941 indicated that 55 percent of the schools in Ohio had radio sets and 66 percent of the schools in California owned radios (Woelfel and Tyler, 1945).

There has been a great deal of speculation about radio's lack of acceptance in the classrooms of the 1930s and 1940s; those speculations offer several potentially interesting messages to CD-ROM proponents. It cannot be assumed that teachers will welcome rich, diverse, and alternative sources of information for their students. Those Depression-era classrooms (many rural and isolated) must have been starved for information, but nobody turned on the radio.

Also, it cannot be assumed that the technological capabilities of any technology will convince schools to use that technology. It is easy to become enraptured with the technical capabilities of a new medium and assume that everybody will share that enthusiasm. Radio must have seemed a technological marvel in the 1930s, but that wasn't enough to convince schools of its educational efficacy. CD-ROM is a technological marvel today as well, but that characteristic alone will not convince today's schools to use the medium.

Price is often cited as one of the barriers to adopting new technologies in the classroom. But apparently radio prices were not prohibitive by the late 1930s when receivers were mass-produced. Even though schools can afford a certain technology, it does not mean that the technology will be used in the classroom.

The most chilling explanation for radio's educational demise (and the most significant lesson for the future success of CD-ROM) was offered by historians Norman Woelfel and Keith Tyler (1945, pp. 4-5). They claimed that the classroom teachers exhibited "indifference and lethargy, even antagonism toward this revolutionary means of communication." Not only was the classroom teacher antagonistic to radio, but the traditional classroom "with its fixed courses of study and rules of conduct couldn't keep pace" (Woelfel and Tyler, 1945, pp. 4-5). The traditional teacher could not "fit" radio into the classroom paradigm and rejected its educational usage—despite the fact that radio technology offered some very real educational benefits. Therefore, future CD-ROM curriculum must be designed so that it "fits" general education.

Educational Television. Educational television received unprecedented funding from private sources in the 1950s and early 1960s; by 1971 more than $100 million had been spent on instructional television by both public and private sources. Television was heralded as the technology that would solve the teacher shortage and improve the nation's curriculum (severely criticized for its supposed inadequacies after the Soviets launched Sputnik).

Educational television received much attention from the media and the public just as it received a great deal of money. But it failed as an educational medium because it was only minimally adopted by the classroom teachers—the "gatekeepers" to the classroom. Today major urban districts often deliver instructional television programs, but these programs are not watched daily by every student. Classroom teachers do occasionally schedule and use specific educational television programs, but in conjunction with and as a supplement to the traditional textbook course of study.

The controversy over why the teachers didn't use the television still rages today. Many researchers point out that the television reformers who conceived, planned, and installed instructional television were nonteachers and were resented by the teaching force. Furthermore, television reformers publicly invited a hostile relationship when they claimed that not only could educational television do many of the same things that teachers did, but that television could do things teachers could not do. The instructional television experience offers a clear lesson that enormous amounts of money cannot ensure a technology's success in education. The experience also seems to indicate that it is best to include educators in the development and integration of any new technology whenever possible. Television proponents didn't further their technology by criticizing teachers and claiming that television was a better instructor than a human teacher.

Computers. Most recently, the public school's integration of computers provides valuable insights about where CD-ROM technology might structurally fit into classrooms. Computers and CD-ROM share at least two characteristics that influence classroom usage patterns. Both are meant to be viewed either by individual students or by a small (two-to four-person) group and both have programs that present information and instructions *independently* of the classroom teacher and thus diminish the teacher's control.

CD-ROM adherents can point to the large number of computers in American schools and argue that classrooms can and did accept technological change dramatically and rapidly. A 1986 Johns Hopkins study showed that a majority of U.S. elementary schools have five or more computers, and that half of U.S. secondary schools have 15 or more computers (Becker, 1986).

CD-ROM will certainly benefit from the numbers of computers already in place in schools and colleges. According to 1986 figures, Apple Computer controlled 53.6 percent of the educational market (Mitgang, 1986). Radio Shack was second with 14.4 percent and Commodore had 10.3 percent. It is not known how many of the Apple and Tandy computers will be compatible with CD-ROM drives. Apple Computer's Martha Steffen (1988) explained that Apple's upcoming CD-ROM drive will be compatible with its IIe and IIGS series as well as the Macintosh line, although the computers will require a special card. The Education Systems Corporation (ECS) runs its CD-ROM-based curriculum on networks of Tandy, Apple IIGS, and IBM computers with a 20-megabyte Macintosh as the master station. However, ECS representative Mary Claire Scanlon explained that most districts purchase new computers when installing her firm's CD-ROM curriculum and do not use computers already in place. ECS offers financing programs to districts, which is often necessary when districts face the $100,000 figure cited by Scanlon as the typical amount that schools spend when implementing ECS (this amount includes 30 computers, a CD-ROM drive, and ECS installation, documentation, and service).

Returning now to the computer experience, CD-ROM technology currently lacks the powerful constituency that prompted education's "computer revolution." The push to use computers in schools came mainly from upper-middle-class parents in suburban communities and in particular from that narrow segment of the population that has particularly high ambitions for themselves and their children (Tucker, 1985). Those parents were responding to society's newly awakened awareness of microcomputers in the early 1980s and were driven by fears that their children would not be able to compete in the workplaces without computer skills. Between 1982 and 1985, parents and PTA members were literally arriving at the schoolhouse door with gift computers in hand. Parents held bake sales, sold raffle tickets and used every other means they could think of to raise the money to buy computers for their children's schools (Tucker, 1985). In many cases, the schools simply didn't know what to do with incompatible systems and software. Finally, many districts were forced to draw up guidelines for computer donations.

The frenzy of education's "computer revolution" was to some extent duplicated in American society. *Time* magazine named the microcomputer the "Machine of the Year" in 1983 in lieu of nominating its usual "Man of the Year." The National Commission on Excellence in Education announced that computing should be treated by the schools as the "fourth r." The computer gained widespread acceptance on two fronts: it became what Pogrow (1983) calls a "cultural technology" (found in a large number of middle and upper socioeconomic families) and a "primary work tool" (a technology that transforms the nature of work).

Needless to say, CD-ROM technology doesn't have an equivalent set of societal advocates to match those of the computer. It is not likely that a CD drive will be *Time*'s cover "man/machine of the year." No influential demographic cohort of parents has emerged to insist that neighborhood schools purchase CD-ROM equipment—nor have any parental groups coalesced to raise funds for the purchase of CD-

ROM. The parental fear that drove education's "computer revolution" hasn't been transferred to any other technology—either videodisc or CD-ROM.

The computer's special-interest group (made up of parents, members of the media, educational technocrats, and politicians, among others) expected that tremendous change would occur when computers were activated inside the classroom. However, teachers reportedly exhibited an "almost instinctive resistance" to the first computers placed in the classroom (Stephenson, 1985). Many practicing teachers simply made explicit or tacit decisions to ignore the technology. But the outside pressure was so great that schools were forced to develop some sort of computer usage patterns. Computer proponents were much more powerful than any proponets that educational radio or television might have had. The computers couldn't stay turned off the way that the radios and the televisions had been.

Yet the massive power vested in education's traditional structure cannot be underestimated. In just a short period of time, two computer usage patterns that did *not* change the traditional classroom configuration emerged and dominated computer-assisted instruction programs in all states. Those patterns are significant for CD-ROM hardware and software developers, because it will be possible to overlay CD-ROM directly onto those computer usage patterns with minimum trouble.

Today, public education uses two basic usage patterns for computer-assisted instruction—neither of which threatens the classroom teacher's control or changes the traditional classroom organization scheme. Students work with computers in one of two ways: (1) special self-contained computer "labs" (outside the normal classroom and with a special instructor); or (2) at an individual "interest center" with a single computer. For those unversed in educational jargon, "interest centers" are workplaces scattered around a classroom, intended for a small number of students, peripheral but related to the curriculum, and are often designed as a reward activity for the student after the regular class work is completed. Therefore, the traditional classroom flow and teaching practices have not been changed by the computers now in place in either the labs or interest centers. Tradition is apparently maintained even in the computer labs. Marc Tucker (1985) found that computer labs usually offer basic skills drill-and-practice software and that the lab teacher usually has to know very little about computers.

Those two usage patterns for computer-based technology can easily be capitalized upon for CD-ROM curriculum. The necessary hardware and software for CD-ROM can be integrated into the computer labs and the interest centers. The problem, of course, is convincing educational decision makers that CD-ROM curriculum surpasses the computer software to such an extent that it is worth the additional investment. One of the obvious benefits that can be easily communicated, and that will particularly appeal to this generation of visually sophisticated students, will be the technology's ability to incorporate extensive graphics within any program. A CD-ROM program can include a graphics sequence that could require 5 to 10 floppy disks.

ECS is the pioneer CD-ROM developer that has convinced at least 300 schools that the technology is a worthwhile investment. And interestingly, ECS's CD-ROM curriculum is networked into classroom interest centers in individual classrooms or into computer labs—paralleling exactly the established computer usage pattern.

IVD. Finally, although adoption is still under way, education's use of videodisc technology is instructive for the CD-ROM industry. In fact, the educational acceptance of CD-ROM may more closely parallel the videodisc experience than it will the computer experience since neither videodisc nor CD-ROM have vocal and powerful parental/societal constituents. These two laser technologies will have to be adopted by education on the basis of their relative educational merits and not because parents, politicians, or reformers mandated their educational usage.

Interactive videodisc curriculum was virtually ignored by the public schools and teacher training colleges for years. The early videodisc proponents were aware of the benefits of Level II and Level III interactivity and concentrated much thought, development, and research in that direction. Level II and Level III videodisc programs are both, generally speaking, computer-driven, a characteristic that removes control from the classroom teacher. The early educational videodisc technocrats thought in terms of individual videodisc-driven workstations for one, two, or three students at the most. But the industrial version of videodisc hardware and software was too expensive for the public schools. More important, this usage pattern left the contemporary teacher in the same position as earlier teachers had been with radio and television: out of control and reduced to a supporting role. The inability to transfer industry's usage pattern of videodisc curriculum to public education was alluded to in an early 1987 interview with WICAT's Chairman of the Board Heuston. He lamented, "We don't see videodisc being used in education for quite a while because of the per workstation cost. . ." (Emerson, 1987, p.23).

However, in a surprise development that gathered momentum in about two years' time (1986-1988), public school teachers initiated a videodisc usage pattern that is both economical and consistent with their traditional large group lecture format. Teachers began to use low-priced videodisc players and various "generic" videodiscs as a source of high-resolution images with which to illustrate their lectures. At the same time, low-cost authoring programs for Apple computers and videodisc players became available and teachers began to sequence the frames from the "generic" videodiscs via the computers and to use the computer-sequenced series of slides during lectures to the entire class. The usage of generic videodisc programs has been much touted as the electronic technology in which the "teacher has control" (Clark, 1984) or "the local district has control" (Pavlonnis, 1987).

Educator Robert Blodgett of California Polytechnic State University described public education's usage pattern in these terms:

> The laser disc is ideal for presentations. . .a teacher can put lecture notes on the computer monitor and use it like a teleprompter, while having the computer call up the appropriate corresponding audiovisual material to illustrate visually the lecture points. For example, when giving a talk on insects, a teacher can read a lecture from the computer monitor while the corresponding slides of insects are shown on the color monitor.
>
> (Blodgett, 1987, p.42)

This usage pattern for videodisc has been well accepted by teachers because it leaves the teacher in control. Interestingly, there have been no documented instances of teachers exhibiting antagonism toward videodisc as they reportedly did toward the radio in the 1940s; nor have teachers displayed the resistance to videodisc technology that they did to computers. The recent upsurge in the sale of videodisc players seems to have gained impetus from teachers themselves. *T.H.E. Report* presented results of a "Plans to Purchase in 1987" survey and estimated that 36,000 videodisc players would be purchased by public schools in 1987, but that figure may be high considering the technological orientation of the journal's readership.

Money is always a concern in the educational field. Therefore, there can be no doubt that videodisc became a viable educational technology only when equipment costs came into line with educational budgets. Prices of videodisc players dropped from $3,500 in 1980 to $590 in 1986 (Pioneer's LD-V2000). Certainly, schools have begun to purchase larger numbers of lower-priced videodisc players and various generic videodisc programs. CD-ROM will not only have to be affordable to education, but also must be perceived as affordable. Many general educators still believe that videodisc technology is prohibitively expensive.

Science is the curricular discipline that makes the most use of videodisc technology; most videodisc projects include a science component. It may be that science teachers are particularly receptive to technology—a question worthy of CD-ROM market research. Or more science videodiscs may be sold simply because there are more science-related videodiscs being marketed by the various vendors. The Minnesota Educational Computing Corporation's (MECC) 1986 *Videodiscs for Education: A Directory* assigns 30 discs to the science discipline, 19 to computer training, 17 to automotive training, and 10 to math.

Videodisc technology is being used by teachers from the early elementary grades through high school primarily as a device to provide high-quality images (both stills and motion video) that relate to the traditional curriculum. CD-ROM cannot deliver motion video and can store only about 9,000 still-frame video images compared with 54,000 frames on a videodisc (Brewer, 1986). But CD-ROM far surpasses videodisc in its ability to combine audio, graphics, still-frame video, and large databases on one disc. Therefore, there need be no head-on competition between these two laser-driven technologies. Instead, CD-ROM and videodisc curriculum could ideally be used together in a complementary fashion that capitalizes on the strengths of both technologies. An overlap could arise if classroom teachers attempt to display graphic material or simulations from a CD-ROM disc to the entire class as part of a lecture. However, CD-ROM will likely face far greater competition from computer software already in place in the computer labs and interest centers than from videodisc technology. Digital video interactive (DVI) and CD-I (compact disc-interactive) will be the technologies that confront videodisc because all three offer motion video and large amounts of high-quality images, those characteristics that prompted educational interest in videodisc when the player prices dropped.

The adaptation that computers and videodisc technology have undergone in the public schools is especially relevant now that CD-ROM technology is poised for development. That adaptation configured the educational use of both computers and videodisc to the traditional classroom pattern and it supports the premise that CD-ROM technology will conform to the traditional classroom.

CD-ROM and Traditional Curriculum

Any type of CD-ROM-based curriculum should coincide with the content of the traditional curriculum already in schools. As has been established, education will either reject or redefine any variables, including curriculum content and structure, that interfere with or complicate established procedures. And the traditional curriculum is well-established at all levels of education—kindergarten through graduate school.

American education divides curriculum into such disciplines as social studies, science, mathematics, and the language arts. Each of these disciplines are then further subdivided into their inherent categories, often called the "key concepts." The tables of contents of textbooks from the major educational publishers are usually listings of the "key concepts" of particular disciplines (subjects) and grade levels. In fact, texts from various publishers often feature the same topics at the same or approximate grade levels. Probably every social studies text from every major publisher features a unit on "the family" in the early primary grades.

The easiest way to align CD-ROM curriculum with established curriculum will be to use the same "key concept" organizers that textbooks are already using. ECS has astutely designed its K-8 CD-ROM curriculum around the traditional concepts in math, reading, and language arts, and is currently developing a science component that will be structured according to the major science concepts already taught in the public schools.

It is not difficult to determine what "key" concepts" are predominant in each subject discipline. Content specialists for the various subjects are on staff at most major universities and can furnish comprehensive outlines describing their respective disciplines' content domains. To use ECS as an example once again, that firm contracts with national experts in math, reading, language arts, and science and solicits their input in order to design the CD-ROM lessons.

Furthermore, ECS sends staff representatives to each school that purchases its curriculum to assist in correlating the 1,800 lessons on the CD-ROM program with that particular school's curriculum scope and sequence. Together, the ECS and school representatives correlate the CD-ROM curricular topics with the school's objectives, the school's standardized text series, and the school's standardized tests.

All CD-ROM firms may not have the staff or resources to work individually with each purchasing school in the future. But it is possible to design and include a cross-referenced teachers' guide with any potential CD-ROM program in any of the subject disciplines. Teachers are already familiar with teachers' guides for the commercial textbook series and a CD-ROM guide could easily supplement the textbook guide.

Certainly, computer software firms have already addressed the need to correlate software with curricular topics. Apple Computer's advertisement in a recent *Education Week* displayed its "Curriculum Software Guides" and explained that manuals matched course needs in math, science, reading, writing, and language skills with the best-rated computer software.

The previously mentioned "Science Helper" CD-ROM program from PC-SIG, Inc., is actually a massive teachers' guide. The program is focused on teachers and is not for student usage (Botsford, 1988). Originally developed at the University of Florida, the program includes 918 lesson plans for science topics commonly encountered in grades K-8. Lesson plans often include recommendations about what supplemental learning materials (i.e., computer software) will best complement each topic. Teachers can print any of the lesson plans from the disc since the material was already in the public domain when it was mastered onto the disc. CD-ROM-based lesson plans for other curricular areas such as math, reading, language arts, and social studies would also be valuable tools for teachers, and the market success of "Science Helper" may give some indication of teachers' receptivity to CD-ROM-based teachers' guides.

But the success of "Science Helper" may not be a good indicator of the future success of other CD-ROM teachers' guides. For as the experience with videodisc courseware suggests, science teachers may be more receptive to new tehcnology than educators in other fields.

Each new technology (motion pictures, radio, television, computers, and videodisc) has arrived with fanfare proclaiming that the technology would replace the textbook in education. In fact, at one early videodisc conference, a speaker went so far as to predict that paper, pencils, perhaps even language, would be rendered obsolete by the videodisc (Daynes, 1984, p. 9). Based upon these past experiences, CD-ROM will not replace textbooks. Instead developers would be best served by designing around the text-based curriculum at this time.

Textbooks are very much a part of the traditional classroom configuration; their significance is both practical and symbolic. The notion of a textbook in a child's hands is a very powerful cultural icon; the image evokes emotional connotations linked to our societal beliefs about childhood. CD-ROM should be linked with texts as an "unprecedented resource" that expands and enhances the content and concepts found in the texts.

Either CD-ROM text or CD-ROM that features audio and graphics can serve as an ideal database resource for use with any text of any curricular discipline. It is obvious that no text can hold the thousands of pages of information stored on a CD-ROM. It is also obvious that no text can diversify its presentation of one concept to include multiple grade levels or different learning styles as is possible with a CD-ROM program. Used together, the textbook and the CD-ROM can meet the needs of the traditional classroom with an extension of the content and delivery modalities that would otherwise be unimaginable. And it appears that education will soon need a diversity of materials, CD-ROM included, to supplement the traditional textbook as the shape of the 1990s classroom emerges.

CD-ROM and Education in the 1990s

Formal education in this country faces incredibly complex problems in the years ahead. A teacher shortage already exists in many areas and is expected to worsen. As the numbers of teachers are dropping, the numbers of students who will need special assistance are rising. Demographics indicate that students in the schools of the near future will be drastically different from students today, with a greater variety of ethnic backgrounds, languages, values, and abilities than ever before (Hodgkinson, 1988).

Public school curriculum of the very near future will have to meet the needs of children in the upcoming school generation who are chararcterized by the following:

- Poverty—currently 24 percent of all children live below the poverty line. This is significant because poverty is one of the greatest indicators of low academic performance
- Non-English speaking—immigration and non-English speaking populations' birthrates have produced large numbers of children who speak minimal or no English. Los Angeles School District already has students who speak 81 different languages and provides "language centers" for students speaking Armenian, Cantonese, Farsi, Khmer, Korean, Philippino, Spanish, and Vietnamese.
- Physical and emotional handicaps—mainstreaming has increased the numbers of handicapped students in regular classrooms and growing instability of the family has increased childhood emotional problems. The phrase "at-risk" is the educational term frequently used to describe students who are not succeeding in school and who have one or more of the three characteristics just listed. Diverse and well-planned curriculum materials are urgently needed to educate the "at-risk" students.

Consider how CD-ROM could be developed as an adjunct to the traditional classroom, but for the purpose of meeting the learning needs of these diverse students. The teacher will still continue lecturing to the class, but the students can have the individual attention they require from CD-ROM programs at either computer labs or in interest centers.

Properly designed CD-ROM programs could offer remedial or advanced lessons for those students achieving above or below the classroom norm. CD-ROM programs in any particular curricular discipline could not only evaluate and place the student at the appropriate level of difficulty, but also offer multiple and varying reiterations of the same concept until the student attained mastery.

Bilingual students (and their teachers) could certainly profit from a classroom version of the CD-ROM-based "Visual Dictionary" developed by Software Mart and Facts on File. The viewer of the "Visual Dictionary" uses a mouse to "click" on a certain object (or section of an object) depicted on the screen and then hears the correct word for that item in either English or French (Steffen, 1988). Such a program could offer translations in the languages of tomorrow's school children, whether that be Spanish, Vietnamese, or Farsi. Both the teacher and the student could use such a program in the effort to develop the student's English language proficiency.

The teacher shortage will result in more students per classroom and, therefore, more students for each teacher. And many of these additional students will be the children with learning problems, little or no English, and physical and emotional handicaps. The teacher is going to be in critical need of assistance.

Theoretically, at least, the students and teachers can benefit from all types of technologies used together in a complementery fashion: computers, videodiscs, CD-ROM, and the future CD-I and DVI.

CD-ROM and Teacher Training

There is one final trend related to the teacher shortage that could prove beneficial for CD-ROM curriculum. Large numbers of new teachers will be needed in the next few years as the present teaching force diminishes in numbers through retirement or career changes. This will be a unique time in history to acquaint large numbers of new teachers with CD-ROM technology. It may be easier to inculcate educational technology usage patterns in teacher trainees when they are in college than to change the practices of teachers who have been in the classrooms for years. If this is the case, educational technology skills may be more easily transferred to significant numbers of tomorrow's teachers who will be attending teacher colleges in the next few years. High-tech firms have subsidized educational technology laboratories in numerous colleges of education over the past few years; the addition of CD-ROM technology to those laboratories should likewise prove to be a worthwhile investment.

At least two CD-ROM products are available that can be integrated into educator preparation programs today. Every student in an educational degree program (teacher training, administrative certification, or graduate research) will at one time or another use education's ERIC (Education Resources Information Center) database and education's *CIJE: Current Index to Journals in Education.* At least three firms are marketing ERIC on CD-ROM: SilverPlatter, DIALOG, and OCLC (Crane, 1987). SilverPlatter is also marketing a CD-ROM disc that includes the

CIJE and the *Resources in Education (RIE)*. Any of these databases would provide an excellent introduction to CD-ROM. To any person who has ever sorted through ERIC's millions of microfiche files, CD-ROM access will seem a wonder. Ideally, each education department would have its own CD-ROM system and its own ERIC and *CIJE* CD-ROM programs. There could not be a better way to introduce nascent educators to CD-ROM than through ERIC and *CIJE*.

But the difference between the ideal for education in the future (whether it be the elementary or graduate school classroom) and the reality will be controlled by one factor: education's traditional shortage of money.

CD-ROM and the Economics of Education

Apple Computer representative Martha Steffen (1988) described education as an "cconomically depressed market." She predicted that the CD-ROM software field will become rife with experimentation and be flooded with so much shareware that it will "take some thinking to make money."

The early pioneers developing computer software faced similar discouragements. According to the executive director of the Carnegie Forum on Education and the Economy, the publishing executives who risked substantial sums on educational computer software development in the early years found that the return on their investment was frequently the loss of their jobs (Tucker, 1985).

Eventually, the microcomputer's powerful societal/parental constituency overrode education's budget constraints. CD-ROM's technology does not have the same powerful groups advocating its educational usage and, therefore, its acceptance into general education will more likely approximate that of videodisc from a financial standpoint. Videodisc has been *slowly* accepted by the public schools, and the acceptance rate has only increased when lower-cost videodisc players came on the market and classroom teachers discovered a means to control videodisc-derived curriculum. The teacher control issue is one that will have to be addressed carefully and thoughtfully by the CD-ROM industry.

Realistically, CD-ROM's future in education will ultimately be tied to the emergence of low-cost hardware and courseware. The videodisc experience has proven that teachers will assist in tailoring a technology to their demands if the cost is low enough and if control can be maintained. The question, of course, is when will the cost be low enough for schools to purchase substantial amounts of CD-ROM drives and courseware? Until that question is answered, the CD-ROM industry should initiate programs to acquaint general education with CD-ROM so that at the beginning of 1989, the majority of educators can answer the question "What is CD-ROM?"

Bibliography

"The Apple Unified School System." *Education Week* (March 23, 1988): 16-17.

Becker, Henry. "Preliminary Results from the New Johns Hopkins Survey." *Classroom Computer Learning* (January 1986): 30-33.

Blodgett, Robert. "Ten Uses of Videodisc in Public Schools." In *Proceedings: National Videodisc Symposium for Education*. Eds. Ward Sybouts and Dorothy Jo Stevens. Lincoln: Division of Continuing Studies of the University of Nebraska, 1987.

Botsford, Chuck. Telephone Interview. April 1988.

Boyer, Ernest. "Why Teachers are the Real Power Behind School Reform." *Instructor* (October 1987): 28-31.

Brewer, Bryan. "Compact Disc Interactive Audio." In *CD ROM The New Papyrus*. Eds. Steve Lambert and Suzanne Ropiequet. Redmond, WA: Microsoft Press, 1986.

Bush, William, and Cobb, Paul. "Using Computers in the Classroom: A Problem for Teacher Educators." *Action in Teacher Education* (Winter 1983-1984): 9-14.

Chilcott, John. "Teachers' and Administrators' Respective World Views." University of Arizona, 1983.

Clark, Joseph. "Videodisc and the Classroom Teacher." Presentation delivered to Association for Supervision and Curriculum Development's curriculum study institute, December 1984.

Combined Proceedings: Optical Disc Read Only Memory Forum, Second Annual Conference on Applications of CD/ROM, Applications of Artificial Intelligence and Expert Systems. Warrenton, VA: Learning Technology Institute, 1987.

Crane, Nancy. "Optical Product Review: DIALOG's OnDIsc ERIC." *CD-ROM Librarian* (July/August 1987): 26-35.

Cuban, Larry. *Teachers and Machines*. New York: Columbia University, 1986.

Darrow, Benjamin. *Radio; The Assistant Teacher*. Columbus, OH: R.G. Adams, 1932.

Daynes, Rod. *The Videodisc Book: A Guide and Directory*. New York: John Wiley and Sons, 1984.

Dede, Christopher. "Empowering Environments, Hypermedia and Microworlds." *The Computing Teacher* (November 1987): 20-24.

Dole, Jan. Telephone Interview. March 1988.

Emerson, L.K. "Q&A." *Instruction Delivery Systems* (May/June 1987): 20-24.

Fox, Raymond. "Technology and the 'Teacher Shortage.'" *SALT Newsletter* (Summer 1987): 1.

Garrison, Chris. Telephone Interview. March 1988.

Gough, Pauline. "A Full Plate." *The Phi Delta Kappan* (March 1988): 466.

Hodgkinson, Harold. "The Right Schools for the Right Kids." *Educational Leadership* (February 1988): 10-14.

Macon, Cynthia. Telephone Interview. April 1988.

Maeroff, Gene. "A Blueprint for Empowering Teachers." *The Phi Delta Kappan* (March 1988): 473-477.

Mitgang, Lee. "Schools in the Computer Age Now Turning to VCRS." *Santa Barbara News Press* (November 1986): G-9, cols. 1-2.

Pavlonnia, Terri. "Integrating Laserdisc Technology into the Curriculum: An Administrator's Point of View." The Annual Nebraska Videodisc Symposium, Lincoln, October 1987.

Pogrow, Stanley. *Education in the Computer Age*. Beverly Hills: Sage Publications, 1983.

Pogrow, Stanley. "On Technological Relevance and the Survival of U.S. Public Schools." *The Phi Delta Kappan* (May 1982): 610-611.

Romberg, Thomas, and Pitman, Allan. *Annual Report to the Ford Foundation: The Urban Mathematics Collaborative Projects*. Madison: University of Wisconsin, 1985.

Scanlon, Mary Claire. Telephone Interview. April 1988.

Steffen, Martha. Telephone Interview. April 1988.

T.H.E. Report (Winter 1987). Irvine, CA: Information Synergy, Inc.

Tucker, Marc. "Computers in the Schools: What Revolution?" *Journal of Communication* (Autumn 1985): 12-23.

U.S. Department of Education. *The 1987 Digest of Educational Statistics* (by Thomas Snyder). Washington, D.C.: Government Printing Office, 1987.

Wilson, Kathleen. "Palenque: The Textbook You'll Use in the Year 2001?" *Instructor* (Fall 1987): 9.

Woelfel, Norman, and Tyler, Keith. *Radio and the School*. Yonkers-on-the-Hudson, NY: World Book Co., 1945.

Wolcott, Harry. *Teachers and Technocrats*. Eugene, OR: Center for Educational Policy and Management, University of Oregon, 1977.

Firms and Representatives Cited in this Chapter

Apple Computer
20525 Mariani Avenue
Cuptertino, CA 95014
408-996-1010
Cynthia Macon
Martha Steffen

Education Systems Corporation
6170 Cornerstone Court
Suite 300
San Diego, CA
619-587-0087
Mary Claire Scanlon

Michigan State University
College of Education
Teacher Education
East Lansing, MI   48864
517-355-1725
Dr. Jan Dole

Microsoft Corporation
16011 NE 36th Way
Box 97017
Redmond, WA   98073
206-882-8080

PC-SIG, Inc.
1030 East Duane Avenue
Sunnyvale, CA   94086
408-730-9292
Chuck Botsford

5

Marketing CD-ROM Technology in the 1980s and 1990s: Business and Retail

MARY ANN O'CONNOR

As companies move out of the research and development stages and into the marketing of CD-ROM products, a number of key issues and concerns arise. Should these products be marketed in the same manner as existing products? If not, what changes should be adopted? What are the markets for these new products? Are these customers the same as those currently purchasing print or online products? What impact will this have on the sales of existing products? How are these new CD-ROM products different from print or online versions? How does a company effectively communicate these differences? How can a company separate the benefits of the technology from the technology itself?

These questions are only a few of those being addressed by companies planning or developing CD-ROM application products. In this chapter these issues and others will be explored and evaluated in terms of what marketing plans are being implemented today. In addition, some speculation about where this technology will be going in the future will contribute to an understanding of how marketing plans must change and evolve to address these future markets.

Introduction

In 1985 the standard specification for CD-ROM was announced by Philips and Sony. Their intention was to produce a modification of the popular CD-DA (compact disc-digital audio) format for the mass distribution of information. The CD-ROM standard specification was designed for use in the computer peripherals marketplace, and CD-ROM was initially targeted at text/data applications in conjunction with personal computers.

When the first hardware and software products began appearing in 1985 it was felt, by many computer professionals, that CD-ROM was a media in search of a market. Today, three years later, some individuals still maintain this position. Is this true? Are the applications currently being marketed on CD-ROM of little interest in the marketplace and will any of the companies currently developing or producing CD-ROM products achieve mass-market acceptance? Although the answers to these questions are as yet undetermined, the number of companies and individuals moving from a position of "wait and see" to that of active participation in the CD-ROM industry is growing at a significant rate.

With the introduction of an increasing number of CD-ROM-based products into the information marketplace, marketing issues and strategies, as they relate to CD-ROM, have become more complex and challenging.

Until fairly recently, marketing efforts focused primarily on education and awareness. These early efforts were somewhat unified in their goal which was to "spread the word" and encourage participation in the industry. Product brochures, trade publications, industry conferences, and prototype demonstrations were all very effective vehicles for communicating the tremendous capabilities and potential for CD-ROM products. They have been highly successful in this regard. The companies that participated in this market during these early days spent significant amounts of money (and time) on marketing with the assumption that there would be little return on their investment for some undetermined amount of time. Unfortunately for some, the educational process was slow and this period of time extended beyond original projections, which required restructuring of marketing strategies and, in a few cases, complete withdrawal from the market.

Digital Equipment Corporation (DEC), an early participant in the CD-ROM industry, initially wished to sell both drives and applications. It solicited database material which was then converted to CD-ROM and marketed by DEC. With a number of publishing-related companies adopting a similar strategy, DEC quickly discovered that its resources were better utilized by focusing on the hardware alone. Although it continues to provide some support and assistance to companies wishing to convert information onto CD-ROM, DEC is now content to sell only the drives.

Two computer peripherals companies, Xebec and Tecmar, also had plans to offer CD-ROM drives. Unfortunately, as early industry participants, they were faced with a number of technological issues that were as yet unresolved. Realizing that research and development efforts would not produce an immediate return, they put their resources into more profitable endeavors.

"The Market," as it was defined in the early days of CD-ROM's introduction, considered application developers primarily as end-users because the hardware had no utility without applications. Today, of course, we are faced with a wide range of hardware and application products that are all seeking "true" end-user acceptance (i.e., customers using CD-ROM products to increase and enhance productivity, irrespective of the technology). This situation creates a unique opportunity to observe a number of marketing plans and strategies and, ultimately, to determine their relative success. Because most CD-ROM application products have been targeted toward vertical markets, these will be the primary focus. The retail marketing of horizontal applications, however, also holds great potential, and early efforts in this area will be discussed as well.

Marketing Plans and Strategies

Approaches to CD-ROM Publishing

One of the very first publishing companies to announce support of CD-ROM, back in 1985, was Reed Publishing, Inc. A subsidiary of Reed, R.R. Bowker Company, released its first CD-ROM application product, Books in Print, in mid-1986. The cost of this CD-based product is roughly four times the printed version (CD-ROM: $895 to $995, print: $250), but Bowker contends this is not only acceptable but justified. Its strategy is to add value to the compact disc product, in the form of searching and browsing and more timely updates than are available in the print version, to justify the incremental cost. This, in itself, presents a marketing challenge with respect to creating awareness among potential customers. Bowker addresses this challenge by focusing its sales efforts on the increased capabilities of the CD-ROM product and going directly to the potential end-user, librarians. Virtually every form of marketing vehicle available is being used, including direct mail, display advertising, trade shows, direct sales force, telemarketing, and special offers. Perhaps the most effective of these will be Bowker's efforts at distributing demonstration diskettes at trade shows and mailing them to potential end-users.

Within the publishing industry, a major concern is that CD-ROM products will erode the sales of existing print products. This has been a serious concern and one that also plagued the interactive videodisc when first introduced around 1980; Bowker does not see this as a problem. Although its print version has a nearly 100 percent penetration within the library market, penetration is not necessarily equated with sales. In this market there exists the phenomena called "pass along copies," a practice in which a main library will pass along out-of-date versions of printed material to its branches while purchasing only one copy of the most updated version for its own use. This means lost sales of the print product. By implementing a CD-ROM strategy that requires the return of outdated discs in order to receive an updated version, Bowker is able to overcome a problem that has long plagued the publishing industry. Only through the introduction of a new media has this solution become feasible.

Another strategy being tested by Bowker is the packaging of more than one product on a single disc. The existence of a strong product on CD-ROM creates an opportunity to bundle less popular products, while providing added value over printed versions of the same products. This strategy has the potential to increase the market penetration of all the products involved.

A different marketing strategy might be to re-package information in a way that would appeal to new markets. For example, NYNEX Information Resources Company is expanding its directory product line by offering NYNEX Fast Track, a white page directory listing on CD-ROM, to specific segments of the business market. Market targets are companies that rely on current, up-to-date address and telephone listings for verification purposes. One application may be credit verification for credit card companies and collection agencies, marketing purposes, telemarketing, and direct mail. Currently, these types of companies must rely on directory assistance for the most up-to-date information, since the printed version is only updated on an annual basis. Companies could also benefit, both financially and in terms of productivity, from having this information in-house. Since the NYNEX disc is a relatively new product, it is too early to tell whether the $10,000 per-year subscription rate is too hefty a price to pay for this convenience.

However, NYNEX is the first to point out that there are a number of packaging alternatives that could lead to greater penetration of other markets and a subsequent reduction in price. An example of this is the Swiss telephone directory which is available in five languages from two companies, one version for approximately $120 and one at a $300 price point. This information has been enhanced through various language offerings and the inclusion of an individual's profession. Unfortunately, a factor that appears to be hindering the sales of these products is the lack of an installed base of drives and the customer's reluctance to purchase a CD-ROM drive for approximately $1,000. (These two topics will be discussed in more detail later in the chapter.)

Another emerging strategy for the penetration of new markets is the formation of strategic alliances. Two examples of this are the Lotus Corporation/Datext Corporation merger and a recent joint venture announcement between Wang Laboratories, Inc., West Publishing Company, and Reference Technology, Inc.

The Lotus/Datext merger provided a company (Lotus) that was already marketing online databases to large corporations with the ability to enhance its product line with CD-ROM technology. At the same time, Datext had already been marketing its line of CD-ROM products to the investment community and clearly saw an association with Lotus as being instrumental toward helping it penetrate the financial segments of large corporations. From all outward appearances, this was truly a marriage made in heaven. According to Lotus president and CEO James Manzi, its CD-ROM business has already reached the $20 million level. Its 1986 revenue from database distribution on CD-ROM was $8.7 million or a mere two-tenths of a percent of its total electronic database revenue. Manzi predicts, however, that by 1990 CD-ROM products will make up 10 percent of total electronic database revenue for his company.

Although these numbers would appear to spell success, no mention of net profit figures have been forthcoming. In fact, comments by David Roux, general manager of Lotus Information Services and former Datext president, indicate that the cost of marketing these products, particularly at their extremely high price points, may reduce profits to a minimum. He also points out that not only are sales very expensive, but support costs are always underestimated. Selling high-technology products in non-technical markets involves not only up-front education, but continuing support as problems and questions arise. This support often requires subject expertise as well as technical competence, thus raising the level of skills required in support personnel and the amount of time spent.

Can these costs be attributed to the applications themselves or are they related to the media? This is a difficult question to answer since the information contained on the CD-ROM products cannot be compared with identical products from either print or online vendors. The compact disc provides the opportunity to make multiple, complementary databases available to end-users, where previously access was available only to one or two databases. Even in situations in which users have had previous access to identical data, the methods used to search and retrieve this information can vary significantly among CD-ROM, online, and print versions. Frequent use and continued familiarity with a product are factors that typically help to reduce the level of support required on a long-term basis. Turnover, changing needs, and the increasing volume of available data, however, may negate these factors. The personal computer industry, for example, keeps many individuals gainfully employed providing support for products such as WordStar and Lotus 1-2-3, in spite of the fact that these products have been around for many years.

The joint venture between Wang, West Publishing, and Reference Technology points out the need for comprehensive marketing approaches. Wang is supplying the hardware, Reference Technology the software, and West Publishing the informational content for a line of CD-ROM products to be offered to the legal market. This triumvirate is currently seeking other strategic partners to enhance this concept. Both Wang and West Publishing have strong marketing positions within the legal community and see the potential for marketing a line of CD-ROM-based products as strategic in terms of future business. Not only do they hope to capitalize upon their ability to sell their own products to their established markets, but they hope to entice other companies into providing components that can expand and enhance their current capabilities. This association literally opens up a channel of marketing and distribution previously unavailable to a wide range of companies. The legal market, although proven to be highly profitable, can be quite difficult to penetrate, particularly with technology-based products.

Retail

No chapter discussing the marketing of CD-ROM products would be complete without the inclusion of marketing through retail. This discussion, so far, has focused on vertical-type applications that use a direct marketing approach. Many industry experts believe that real success in the CD-ROM industry will involve mass-market acceptance. The main proponents of this belief, of course, already participate in the mass market. Considering the high cost of development for CD-ROM products (in many cases well over a million dollars for a single product), companies must look to high-volume sales in order to recover this expense and begin to see a profit. Few vertical markets, even at high penetration levels, can provide sales of this magnitude. One alternative to this problem is to offer products at higher prices. This choice, however, limits penetration and consequently has the same effect on profitability.

The first truly horizontal application was introduced by Microsoft Corporation in 1987. Marketed in conjunction with a hardware manufacturer, Amdek Corporation, Microsoft Bookshelf brought CD-ROM technology to retail outlets for the first time. The retail channel, however, is filled with employees who have limited knowledge about many of the products on the market. The introduction of a new technology usually involves a commitment to retail employee education and training before results can be seen. Recent announcements by Apple Computer, Inc. (its introduction of a CD-ROM drive under its own label) and Tandy Corporation's (Radio Shack) impending distribution of CD-ROM drives indicate even greater penetration of the retail channels. However, no mention, in either of these announcements, has been made of efforts to communicate the benefits of CD-ROM technology to the individuals who will be responsible for transferring that information to real customers.

In the early 1980s IBM Corporation faced a similar challenge when it introduced its personal computer through retail channels for the first time. In typical IBM fashion, the company spent considerable time and money studying the environment and soliciting feedback from retail personnel. Unique new marketing plans, including extensive training programs, were implemented, and we have all witnessed their tremendous success. Perhaps Apple Computer will be the catalyst it claims to be and will make the marketing commitment necessary to stimulate retail sales of CD-ROM technology. Clearly, a broad range of application products (e.g., CD-ROM discs and software), which have wide appeal to personal computer users, will be required before interest in the hardware can be stimulated. Additionally, end-users should not have to experience technical problems, such as how to extend operating system capabilities to accommodate CD-ROM, when they purchase the hardware and/or applications. As the Microsoft CD-ROM extensions become standard with the purchase of most CD-ROM drives, this problem will be overcome in the IBM-PC environment.

One approach to the development of a broader base of application products might be to look for horizontal applications within the base of existing vertical products. Perhaps many applications with vertical origins, such as financial and business reference databases, could be sold at retail. Microsoft has demonstrated its belief in this concept by introducing two new products: StatPack and Small Business Consultant. These products are based on information sources not typically used by smaller organizations. By repackaging this information and offering it at attractive prices ($150) Microsoft hopes to penetrate the small business market.

A problem that will plague the retail environment for some time is the lack of an installed base of CD-ROM drives. Few people will buy the drive as a novelty, particularly at a $1,000 or greater price point. Instead, consumers will be seeking practical, useful applications. This means that developers must spend precious development funds (and other resources) on the hope that their application will be the one to drive the market.

Now that Apple Computer and Radio Shack have also entered the market, applications developers are faced with a real dilemma: Should they develop for the IBM-PC and compatibles market with around 50,000 CD-ROM drives already sold, or should they take a chance on the Apple or Radio Shack computers with no base of drives at all? Several companies are hedging their bets by producing products for all three. This dilemma is not new and is primarily responsible for the limited number of personal computer manufacturers that are not IBM-

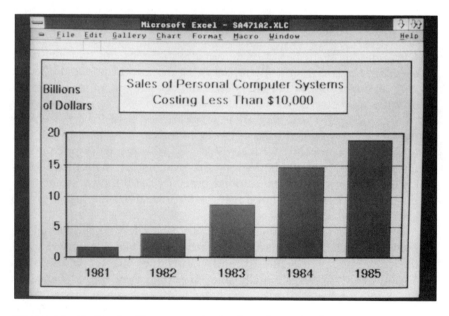

Agricultural Statistics, 1985 (Search)

Edit   View   Search   Browse   Options   Next   Previous   Help

Table 686.--Per capita consumption of major food commodities (retail
weight), United States, 1977-85{1}*

Commodity	1977	1978	1979	1980	1981	1982	1
	Pounds	Pounds	Pounds	Pounds	Pounds	Pounds	Pou
Meats	152.3	146.9	144.8	147.7	145.1	139.3	14
Beef	91.8	87.2	78.0	76.5	77.1	77.2	7
Veal	3.2	2.4	1.7	1.5	1.6	1.7	
Lamb and mutton	1.7	1.6	1.5	1.5	1.6	1.7	
Pork	60.5	60.3	68.8	73.5	69.9	62.7	6
Fish (edible weight)	12.7	13.4	13.0	12.8	12.9	12.3	1
Canned	4.6	5.0	4.8	4.5	4.8	4.3	
Fresh and frozen	7.7	8.1	7.8	8.0	7.8	7.7	
Cured	.4	.3	.4	.3	.3	.3	
Poultry products:							
Eggs	34.0	34.6	35.3	34.6	33.8	33.4	3
Chicken	44.1	46.7	50.6	50.1	51.7	53.1	5

Figure 20. StatPack replaces volumes of reference material with a single CD-ROM disc. Courtesy Microsoft Corporation.

Microsoft Excel - SA471A2.XLC

File   Edit   Gallery   Chart   Format   Macro   Window   Help

Billions
of Dollars

Sales of Personal Computer Systems
Costing Less Than $10,000

20

15

10

5

0

1981   1982   1983   1984   1985

Figure 21. StatPack allows users to load and manipulate statistics into applications such as Microsoft Excel and Lotus 1-2-3. Courtesy Microsoft Corporation.

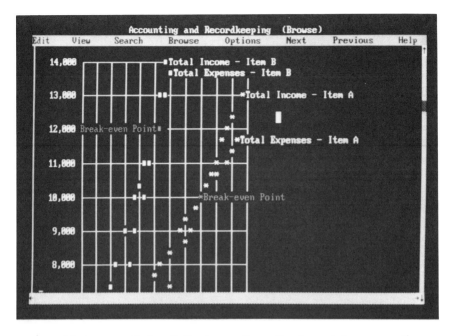

Figure 22. Microsoft Small Business Consultant contains more than 220 publications on topics ranging from accounting to importing and exporting. Courtesy Microsoft Corporation.

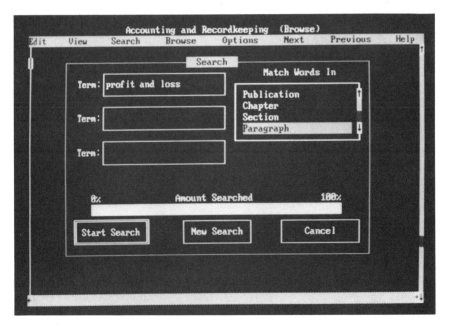

Figure 23. Users can perform keyword searches using Miicrosoft Small Business Consultant. Courtesy Microsoft Corporation.

PC compatible. Without support from the application development community, a hardware developer cannot survive. Apple Computer and Radio Shack are both attempting to attract developers of existing CD-ROM products. The cost of converting an application onto a new computer base is obviously less than that of creating a new application. Their hope, therefore, is to be able to compete with a number of like CD-ROM application offerings in order to build an installed base of their own. Apple Computer also hopes to attract developers with increased hardware capabilities by promoting HyperCard and the Macintosh user interface.

A unique marketing approach is being taken by Aries Systems Corporation. Knowing that at least two versions of the MEDLINE database were already available on CD-ROM for IBM personal computers and compatibles, it chose to offer MEDLINE for the Macintosh computer in an attempt to carve out a niche in the market for itself. (See Chapter 2 for a comparison of eight CD-ROM MEDLINE products including the Aries' Macintosh system.) Aries' marketing strategy includes selling through dealers and agents and approaching professional societies to solicit their participation. This is a vertical application, however; the firm is using a combination of direct marketing and retail in the hopes that this will afford it greater penetration in the medical and health care markets. Aries indicates, however, that its problem is not only the lack of an installed base of CD-ROM drives but also a lack of Macintosh users.

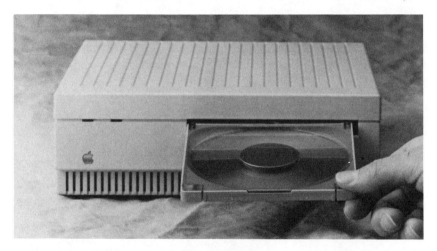

Figure 24. The AppleCD SC is a front-loading drive that allows it to be stored above or below the computer without taking up additional desk space. It features a small computer systems interface (SCSI) that allows it to work with both the Macintosh and Apple computer families. Courtesy Microsoft Corporation.

CD-ROM Products for the AppleCD SC CD-ROM Drive

Company	*Product*
Facts on File, Inc.	Facts on File News Digest CD-ROM Public Domain Software on File
Bowker Electronic Publishing	Books in Print *Plus*
Grolier Electronic Publishing, Inc.	Americana Series (sampler of U.S. history 1800-1850) The Electronic Encyclopedia
Highlighted Data, Inc.	Electronic Map cabinet Merriam-Webster's Ninth New Collegiate Dictionary
Multi-Ad Services, Inc.	Kwikee INHOUSE Pal (art library on CD-ROM)
Optical Media International	Sound Designer Universe of Sounds, Volumes I and II
Whole Earth Review	The Whole Earth Learning Disc
Personal Bibliographic Software, Inc.	Interface compatibility for PBS CD-ROM products
Aries Systems Corporation	Interface compatibility for ASC's CD-ROM products

---

McGraw-Hill, which plans to publish the Sweet's Catalog on CD-ROM in January of 1989, is also anticipating a problem with its installed base. Believing that placing its CD-ROM product in the hands of a strategic set of end-users will help to sell its market, McGraw-Hill plans to place 33,500 copies of the disc into design/construction sites within the construction industry. It expects that only 100 to 200 of these sites will have CD-ROM drives by that time (January 1989). In order to stimulate hardware sales, it will offer low pre-publication prices for CD-ROM drives, strong promotion programs, and possibly post-publication rebate coupons. The firm has committed $1 million in sales and marketing efforts to cover the period of May through December in anticipation of the release of this product. Fortunately for McGraw-Hill, its potential customer base is nearly 90 percent computerized and 85 percent of those have IBM personal computers or compatibles. Having accurate data such as this about a potential market can help to keep development and marketing costs at a minimum, and makes a strong case for either staying within an established market or developing a strategic relationship with a firm already established in an identified market.

Future Marketing Efforts

Having reviewed current and past CD-ROM marketing activities, the question arises: what further marketing efforts are needed now and in the future? What conditions must exist in order for those efforts to be effective?

First it is necessary to examine the hardware situation. Clearly, there are many alternative CD-ROM drive products, such as those available from Philips, Sony, and Hitachi. Enough manufacturers are now participating in this market to allow freedom of choice for end-users. Freedom of choice, however, usually includes some variation in price and corresponding functionality. The nature of a CD-ROM drive and the standards governing the disc itself prevent much variation in functionality and, unfortunately, we have seen little variation in price. Although some applications vendors are selling drives for as little as $680 when packaged with their application products, the typical cost of an IBM-PC-compatible CD-ROM drive is closer to the $1,000 price point. The new Apple drive will retail for a suggested list price of $1,199. Atari is planning a CD-ROM drive at around $600, but it is not yet available. Many people believe that to achieve true success, the CD-ROM drives must come down in price.

The real issue here is not the price of the drive but, rather, the value a customer places upon the application that requires the drive. For individuals who place a high value on the ability to view (and/or record) entertainment in the privacy of their home, $1,000 is a reasonable price to pay for a VCR. For others, this price is prohibitive. Mass-market penetration requires a combination of both utility and pricing.

Nearly 50,000 sales, to date, at $1,000 per drive, does not indicate a totally prohibitive price at this stage of market development. It is safe to expect and assume that this price will decrease as competition and sales increase. Looking at the acceptance of hard disk drives in the personal computer market, one can draw some inferences concerning price points. When the price of a 20-megabyte hard disk drive exceeded the $1,000 mark (as recently as three years ago), real need (volume of data to be stored) was the primary determinate in the purchase of the drive. Today, with prices as low as $300, 20-megabyte hard disk drives have become standard equipment on most personal computers.

Pricing, in terms of applications, becomes a more complex issue. Taking an existing print or online application and enhancing it for CD-ROM appears to be a sound approach for entry into the CD-ROM market. The question becomes: What are those enhancements worth? One fear, held by CD-ROM supporters, is that developers will use the novelty of CD-ROM to sell empty enhancements and CD-ROM will become an acronym for "Compact Disc-Really Outrageous Money." The point here is that developers must be able to show potential customers *real value* in the new CD-ROM application and that value must coincide with the increase in price. Some publishers believe that high prices for their CD-ROM applications will protect them from eroding the sales of existing print or online products. However, this philosophy goes against one of the main benefits of implementing CD-ROM which is the ability to achieve economies through scale. If too many publishers adopt this approach, then we can expect that a significant number of CD-ROM products will remain on the shelf and the CD-ROM industry will never achieve its true potential.

Suggestions concerning the added-value issue include soliciting input from potential customers and/or extending the search for innovation into the marketplace. This means that the large corporations that are currently responsible for the majority of CD-ROM development efforts might need to coordinate these efforts with those of smaller companies and individuals. This can only be accomplished by reducing development costs and making more tools, such as authoring systems, available and at affordable prices. Developers and industry experts agree that the potential for CD-ROM and related products spans many markets. Again, the only way in which many of these markets can be tapped is through the efforts of a large number of individuals and companies. Large corporations (and government) typically spend huge amounts of money on development and, consequently, must seek large markets to recover these expenses. Small, special niche markets are often overlooked and, thus, some truly creative products and tools may be a long time in coming.

Recently, several companies have started offering their products and/or services at a lease or per-hour basis to smaller companies. Special offers in the area of mastering and replication to encourage prototype development is another approach that may be effective in reducing development costs. Apple Computer is planning to offer a Starter Kit to prospective developers that will allow them to ship an application to Apple on a hard disk and receive 100 CD-ROM discs in return. The details of this offer, including pricing, are still being worked out. As yet, however, development for CD-ROM remains very expensive and highly speculative.

Because CD-ROM was originally positioned as a vehicle that could hold massive amounts of information, the library market became the target of many application developers. (See Chapter 1 for an examination of the library market.) Eventually, however, the number of libraries and the financial resources available to them made it clear that the potential for this market is indeed limited, and that marketing efforts needed to be expanded to include other, more lucrative areas. The library industry holds significant appeal for CD-ROM developers because of the belief that a large percentage of the installed CD-ROM drive base now resides in this market. Selling to an installed base is far easier than penetrating a new market with new technology. Recent data presented by Microsoft, however, indicates that 90 percent of the installed base of CD-ROM drives is in business and government and only 10 percent is in libraries. Although this data corrects certain impressions concerning the library market, it should not be interpreted in terms of opportunity. Because new technology is initially purchased by research departments and individuals seeking innovation, this data can be misleading. Distribution statistics in the early days of a new technology are not necessarily representative of future trends.

Computer retail outlets are seeking commercial applications since this is the majority of their business. A strong relationship exists between the type of products that are used for reference in a library and the type of products that businesses could use. After all, not every business can afford the luxury of a professional researcher or in-house librarian for its informational needs.

Additional issues that will affect both development efforts and marketing include the enhancement of products with graphics, video, and sound, the increased use of networks, and the new high performance computers and operating systems. As companies convert to new technologies, they will look for product support for these increased capabilities.

Where marketing efforts over the past three years focused on education and industry participation, the emphasis today must be on product sales. With development costs running in the millions of dollars, return on investment is becoming a primary concern, particularly for companies that have been participating in the industry for three years or more. An obvious approach appears to be to match development dollars with equal marketing dollars. This seems to do little to relieve the financial situation, but may prove to be effective as it did in the early days of Lotus 1-2-3, when no one firm had been able to take market share away from the popular spreadsheet program Visicalc.

Are we really looking to take market share away from anybody in this case? Probably not. We are looking to establish a market and that takes time. John Sculley, president and CEO of Apple Computer, points out that it typically takes as long as 15 years for technology to transfer from the lab to the marketplace. Feedback from the user community indicates that where CD-ROM products provide true value-added capability (additional information, quicker searches, etc.) compared with alternative information sources, and this utility is effectively communicated, customer acceptance is forthcoming. Effective communication may be nothing more than a demonstration on floppy disk or the ability to try a product on a free, money-back, trial basis. If a manufacturer has real confidence in a product, there is no risk associated with this approach. If the product, however, is twice as hard to use as the printed equivalent and takes three times as long to use, then no marketing effort will prove successful.

New CD Formats: Impact on and Implications for the CD-ROM Market

Just when compact discs are starting to become familiar to the general public, the industry is becoming clouded with emerging variations of the CD format: CD-I, CD-V, ICVD, DVI. Are these new formats competitive, complementary, or just plain disruptive to the compact disc industry? Again, it is too early to tell. However, some comments related to their relative positioning and market expectations are appropriate to this discussion.

Philips and Sony, responsible for the CD-Audio, CD-ROM, and CD-I (compact disc-interactive) standard specifications, are faced with considerable challenges with respect to relative positioning of these products. CD Audio is obviously a consumer entertainment product; CD-ROM has been positioned as a vehicle to provide information to the business/government/industrial segments. CD-I, the newest development, is also being positioned as a consumer product, to bring "interactive" information into the home to entertain, educate, and inform. Of course, Philips and Sony could not be expected to continue to dominate the compact disc industry indefinitely. With the introduction of the digital video interactive (DVI) format by GE/RCA in early 1987, competition for one or more of the above markets began. The DVI product literally spans all markets and the individuals responsible for the marketing of this new format appear to be open to penetrating one or all of them.

A third format, ICVD (interactive compact videodisc), is also being positioned as a product for many markets. However, because it was not developed within and supported by a major corporation (Mattel Corporation licensed this format for a new generation of toys), it may not be as effective in attracting application developers and thus may have difficulty competing.

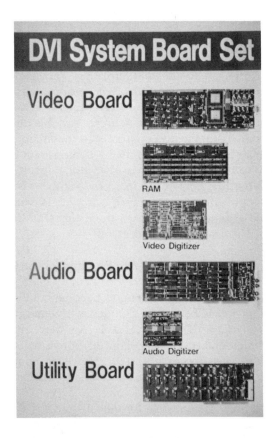

Figure 25. © GE/DVI Technology Venture.

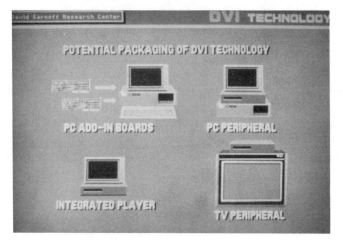

Figure 26. © GE/DVI Technology Venture.

Figure 27. Final elevation screen from DVI design and decorate application. © General Electric Company and Videodisc Publishing, Inc.

Figure 28. Sample of what a DVI landscaping application may look like.

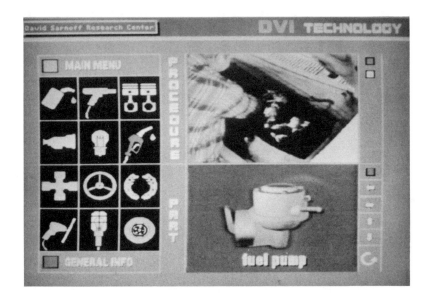

Figure 29. Sample of what a DVI auto repair training application might look like. © General Electric Company.

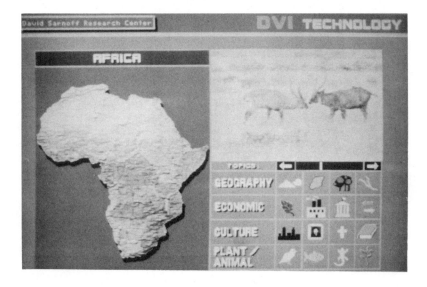

Figure 30. Sample of what a DVI geography teaching application might look like. © General Electric Company.

Any speculation concerning CD-I, DVI, and ICVD, and their relative success in any market, can be based only upon the applications being developed for them. Through a series of joint ventures and support programs sponsored by Philips, the direction of application development for CD-I has been somewhat controlled. Keeping a clear focus on the consumer market, strategic relationships have been formed that are intended to provide a broad range of application products at the time of hardware availability. This may be enough to ensure domination of this market if timing does not become a problem. Originally planned for a 1987 launch, CD-I is not yet available and beginning to feel pressure from other manufacturers. The development of authoring tools and systems is also behind schedule and will have an impact on application availability.

The manufacturers of DVI have just begun their application development support programs and it is too early to tell their direction. It appears, however, that GE/RCA is willing to talk to any firm or individual who has a potential DVI application. Whether these efforts will leave them too diverse and unfocused, and what effect this will have upon the ultimate success of the product, is anybody's guess. It would appear, though, that covering several markets would be a safer bet than to focus all efforts on the highly speculative mass consumer market.

Another advantage that DVI has over CD-I is that it is based on IBM-PC architecture, something with which most developers are familiar. The CD-I system, on the other hand, is based on a system architecture that, if not new to many developers, is certainly not off-the-shelf. The CD-I operating system is a derivative of the OS/9 system, one that is not in wide use.

When these new formats move out of the education and involvement stages of marketing, the companies involved will be faced with marketing to end-users. Currently, too much emphasis is being placed upon the hardware and the media (compact disc). When these products reach the general public the emphasis must be placed upon utility and not technical details. Although this may sound somewhat basic, a surprising number of companies overlook the obvious. The CD-ROM products that appear to be achieving the greatest levels of success, in today's terms, are those that appeal directly to the end-users. Hands-on demonstrations, sample copies of discs, and field tests are all vehicles that should be used to communicate the benefits available through compact disc technology.

With these new formats has come the ability to enrich and enhance applications through the use of graphics, sound, and video. This ability will allow application developers full use of their creative talents. Regardless of the technology, this has to be good news for the consumer. Depending upon how these applications are implemented, a situation may develop in which all compact disc formats are coexisting and have created unique new markets of their own.

Recordable and Erasable Optical Disks

A word about write-once and erasable compact disks must be included for those who still believe that CD-ROM and other read-only formats have a limited life span.

When discussing WORM (write-once, read-many) disks, two issues usually arise. First, why would anyone want a read-only disc that requires a mastering process when they can have a write-once disk that can be prepared on a basic personal computer system? Current 5 1/2-inch WORM disks (roughly the size of a compact disc) have no compatibility with any of the CD formats. Once an application has been placed upon a WORM disk, it can only be distributed to users with a compatible drive. Considering that existing WORM drives cost $2,500 and up, this would indicate a very limited base. For this reason, WORM technology is best suited to environments that have limited distribution. This means internal archiving of information or the distribution of information inside an organization.

There is, however, a proposed standard from Philips and Sony for a WORM disk that will have some limited compatibility with CD-ROM. Although an existing CD-Audio or CD-ROM drive would not be able to play this WORM disk, the WORM drive would be able to play CD-Audio and CD-ROM discs. This would somewhat overcome the concept of a "single-purpose" drive. From a marketing standpoint, a compatible WORM drive has tremendous potential in business and other markets where there is a need to both store internal information and access information being distributed from outside sources.

Unfortunately, this proposed format points out the other issue related to WORM discs, and that is the ability to copy, or download information from a CD-ROM to a WORM disk. Although the debate about copying information could go on forever, is this situation really any different from the early days of photocopy machines? Copying copyrighted information, whether it be in printed or electronic format, is going to occur, regardless of the availability of a specific product. A WORM drive that provides the ability to access pre-recorded data, as well as store internal information, has considerable potential in an age where people are involved in a daily struggle to control the volumes of information surrounding them. Although efforts in the area of copy protection and encryption have been somewhat unproductive to date, the potential for write-once disks should encourage continued research.

Developments in the area of erasable disks indicate that some of the same problems will be encountered, at least initially. The success of CD-Audio is so obviously linked to the standard specifications and compatibility between drives that independent efforts to develop write-once and erasable disks, without the benefit of these standards, could lead to products with little market appeal. While everyone will agree that the ability to store massive amounts of data on an erasable disc may be advantageous, having a number of incompatible drives from which to choose from, at high prices, may outweigh the perceived benefit for some time.

Conclusion

What does the future hold for CD-ROM? With so much effort going into research one can hardly imagine the choices that will have to be made with respect to future products. The ability to store massive amounts of information provides options never before possible. Work being conducted in the areas of artificial intelligence, expert systems, erasable discs, and optical scanners allows us to speculate about capabilities not now imaginable. It is too easy to lose sight of what can be accomplished today when futuristic scenarios are constantly being presented. It is as if we get so inured to new technological developments that we "devalue" our present day capabilities and opportunities.

The marketing environment, however, quickly brings us back to reality. The only truly effective marketing strategies are those that focus on today's capabilities and smooth, effective transitions into the future. It is a small market segment that spends money on technology for technology's sake and few businesses can survive on products that have a short life span; CD-ROM will be a survivor.

Perhaps the CD-ROM drive of today will evolve to encompass more and more formats (CD-I, DVI, WORM, erasable, etc.). However, the basic underlying benefits will remain. Once end-users have discovered the one application on a CD-ROM disc that changes work or personal habits, they will be hooked. This has been true with automobiles, personal computers, and CD-Audio. Of course, that one application will not be the same for everyone, but compact disc and its various forms place no limits upon the variety and richness of future products. Just as automobiles, dishwashers, and stereo equipment can be upgraded for new, more enhanced models, personal computers and CD-ROM drives will be upgraded to take advantage of new technological and application developments.

How can any of us, as consumers, resist the temptation of this technology? All that remains is the time, resources, and communication necessary to turn this blossoming technology into a mainstream industry.

Contact Information

Apple Computer, Inc.
20525 Mariani Avenue
Cupertino, CA 95014
408-996-1010
John Sculley, chairman and CEO

Aries Systems Corporation
79 Boxford Street
North Andover, MA 01845-3219
Lyndon Holmes, president

Digital Equipment Corporation
Ten Tara Boulevard
Nashua, NH 03062-2802
603-884-5111
Ed Schmid, marketing manager

General Electric Digital Video Interactive Technology
David Sarnoff Research Center
CN5300
Princeton, NJ 08543–5300
609-734-2211

Lotus Development Corporation
55 Cambridge Parkway
Cambridge, MA 02142
David Roux, general manager, CD-ROM Information Services

McGraw-Hill Information Systems Company
1221 Avenue of the Americas
20th floor
New York, NY 10020
Hugh Sharp, W.P., Product Planning and Development

Microsoft Corporation
16011 N.E. 36th Way
Redmond, WA 98073
206-882-8080

Nynex Information Resources
100 Church Street
Room 945
New York, NY 10007
Doug Cummings, manager, Business Development

Philips International B.V.
Building SEH-3
5600 MD Eindhoven
The Netherlands

Reed Publishing
275 Washington Street
Newton, MA 02158
Peter Urbach, vice president

Reference Technology, Inc.
5700 Flatiron Parkway
Boulder, CO 80301
John Einberger, vice president, Software Development

Wang Laboratories, Inc.
1 Industrial Avenue
M/S 014-A7a
Lowell, MA 01851
Ri Regina, senior product manager

West Publishing Company
50 West Kellogg Boulevard
P.O. Box 64526
St. Paul, MN 55164-0526
Chares Shapiro, manager, WESTLAW Special Projects

Appendix: Brief Description of CD-ROM Technology and References to Standards

CD-ROM: What Is It and How Does It Work?

This appendix provides the reader with a summary of CD-ROM characteristics and features, a brief description of how the technology works and the CD-ROM standard. The reader is referred to Chapter 2 in *The Essential Guide to CD-ROM* by Roth, et al., and *Memory and Storage*, a volume in the Time-Life Books series on Understanding Computers, for more in-depth and technical descriptions and discussions of CD-ROM technology.

CD-ROM Characteristics and Features

Based upon the compact disc-digital audio (CD-DA) disc technology, a CD-ROM disc is a read-only optical storage format introduced in early 1985. The CD-ROM disc is small (4.7 inches in diameter), relatively rugged, and heat and scratch-resistant.

A single CD-ROM disc can store the equivalent of 800 eight-inch floppy disks, 200 books each containing 1,000 pages, 10 computer magnetic tapes, 1,500 5.25-inch floppy diskettes, or 275,000 pages of text. The storage capacity of a single disc is 15 billion bits of computer data which translates into about 600 megabytes.

A CD-ROM disc can serve as a text-only database, or as a multimedia database storing audio, graphics, photographic images, and digital data.

How CD-ROM Works

Data is stored on the disc as a spiral track of microscopic pits. Machine-readable information is stored on the disc as a series of pits (data) and lands (no data) that spiral to form the area from the center of the disc to its outer edge. When inserted into a CD-ROM drive or CD player, these microscopic pits appear as bumps from beneath the disc and scatter the light from the laser beam. Lands, the areas between the pits, reflect the light from the laser.

Intermittent bursts of light are deflected onto light-detector laser diodes through light polarization techniques that convert the light into electronic signals and decode them as on-off binary bits—ones and zeros.

There are two possible transitions: land-to-pit or pit-to-land. A string of zeros is generated by the path length between these two transitions. Combinations of ones and zeros are grouped in 14-bit long strings that, by matching them against data tables that are stored in permanent memory chips in the CD-ROM drive, are decoded into eight-bit data symbols. In order to appreciate its compactness, consider that the disc's entire spiral data track is almost three miles long, and each individual data track is 1.2 micrometers, which is one-sixtieth the width of a human hair. These tracks are separated by 1.6 micros. Each separate microscopic pit is about 0.5 micrometers wide by 2 micrometers long and has a depth measurement of 0.1 micrometers.

CD-ROM drives read the information contained on the disc by focusing low-powered laser beams on the microscopic pits. An optical unit measures the pits' reflectivity and the CD-ROM drive's semiconductor translates that reflectivity back into a binary signal that can be read by a computer.

Standards

The International Standards Organization (ISO) 9660 Volume and File Structure of CD-ROM Information Interchange (ISO 9660 CD-ROM Standard) is a single international CD-ROM standard. ISO 9660 allows users of information processing systems in conformance with ISO 9660 to mount and read any ISO 9660-conforming CD-ROM disc.

Originating from a proposal to the ISO by the High Sierra Group, an ad hoc group of vendors including DEC, Apple, Hewlett-Packard, Philips, Sony, and in cooperation with NISO (National Information Standards Organization), the American body responsible for developing the formal standard, this standard is expected to go far in encouraging an international market for CD-ROM applications. A common blueprint around which to build worldwide-compatible CD-ROM products is one of the possibilities offered by the ISO 9660 standard. For a copy of ISO 9660, write to Patricia Harris, National Bureau of Standards, NISO, Gaithersburg, MD 20760 (301/921-3241).

See Working Paper for Information Processing: Volume and File Structure of CD-ROM for Information Interchange, and Review and Commentary on the Working Paper in Issue 7:1 of *Optical Information Systems* for the working documents upon which ISSO 9660 is based. The Working Paper for Information Processing: Volume and File Structure for Information Interchange was developed by the CD-ROM Ad Hoc Adivsory Committee (popularly known as the High Sierra

Group), an ad hoc committee representing service companies, vendors, and manufacturers serving the optical disk industry. The Review and Commentary is based on comments, questions, and discussion which took place at the July 14-15, 1986 meeting of NISO Standards Committee EE as the Committee reviewed the Working Paper. It was made available to aid in understanding the technical matters presented in the High Sierra Proposal. See also *CD-ROM Standards: The Book* by Julie Schwerin for an in-depth analysis of the CD-ROM standard.

Information Resources

Befeler, Michael F. "Laserdisc Systems from Reference Technology: Multi-user Technology for High-Use Environments." *Library Hi Tech* 3:2 (1985): 55-59.

Bowers, Richard A. "Making A Living Off the Government." *CD-ROM Review* (January/February 1988): 34-37.

Bowers, Richard A. *Optical Publishing Directory*. Second Edition. Medford, NJ: Learned Information, 1987.

Brewer, Bryan. "Getting 'It' to Happen." *CD-ROM Review* (March/April 1988): 26-29.

Buddine, Laura. *Brady Guide to CD-ROM.* New York, NY: Prentice Hall, 1987.

CD-ROM: The New Papyrus/The Video. Available in VHS and BETA. Developed in conjunction with the First International Conference on CD-ROM in March 1986. Seattle, WA: Microsoft Press, 1986.

Cohen, Elaine, and Young, Margo. "Cost Comparison of Abstracts and Indexes on Paper, CD-ROM, and Online." *Optical Information Systems* 6:6 (November/December 1986): 485-490. Meckler Corporation, Westport, CT.

Davis, Susan. *CD-ROM: Technology and Applications.* White Plains, NY: Knowledge Industry Publications, Inc., 1986.

Desmarais, Norman. *The Librarian's CD-ROM Handbook.* Meckler Corporation, Westport, CT, 1988.

———. "Laserbases for Library Technical Services." *Optical Information Systems* 7:1 (January/February 1987): 57-61. Meckler Corporation, Westport, CT.

Helgerson, Linda. *CD-ROM Sourcebook.* Falls Church, VA: Diversified Data Resources, Inc., 1986.

———. *CD-ROM Sourcedisc.* Falls Church, VA: Diversified Data Resources, Inc., 1988.

Gale, John. "The Information Workstation: A Confluence of Technologies Including the CD-ROM." *Information Technology and Libraries* 4:2 (1985): 137-139.

———. "Organizations Hash Out CD-ROM Standards, Compatiblity Issues." *Computerworld* (August 24, 1987): 67-68.

———, with Clifford A. Lynch and Edwin B. Brownrigg. *CD-ROM Software: Textual Retrieval and Networking Issues—A Research Report.* Boston, MA: Institute for Graphic Communication, 1988.

Giles, Peter. "Optical Disk Applications: Now That We Have Them—What Are They Good For?" *IMC Journal* (July-August 1987): 22-23.

Interactive Multimedia: Visions of Multimedia for Developers, Educators, and Information Providers. Edited by Sueann Ambron and Kristina Hooper. Seattle, WA: Microsoft Press, 1988.

Miller, David C. *Special Report: Publishers, Libraries and CD-ROM: Implications of Digital Optical Printing.* DCM Associates, Portland, OR and American Library Association, Chicago, IL.

———. "Evaluating CD-ROMs: To Buy or What to Buy?" *Database* 10:3 (1987): 36-42.

Miller, Tim. "Early User Reaction to CD-ROM and Videodisc-Based Optical Information Products in the Library Market." *Optical Information Systems* 7:3 (May/June 1987): 205-209. Meckler Corporation, Westport, CT.

Murphy, Brower. "Libraries and CD-ROM. A Special Report." *Small Computers in Libraries* 5 (April 1987): 7-10. Meckler Corporation, Westport, CT.

Nelson, Nancy Melin. *Essential Guide to the Library IBM-PC: Library Applications of Optical Disk and CD-ROM Technology, Volume 8.* Meckler Corporation, Westport, CT.

———. *CD-ROMs in Print 1987.* Westport, CT: Meckler Corporation, 1987.

Newhard, Robert. "Converting Information into Knowledge: The Promise of CD-ROM." *Wilson Library Bulletin* 62:4 (1987): 36-38.

O'Connor, Mary Ann. "Education and CD-ROM." *Optical Information Systems* 6:4 (July/August 1986): 324-331. Meckler Corporation, Westport, CT.

Philips International Inc. (Netherlands). *Compact Disc-Interactive: A Designer's Overview.* New York: McGraw-Hill, 1988.

Pooley, Christopher. "The CD-ROM Marketplace: A Producer's Perspective." *Wilson Library Bulletin* 62:4 (1987): 24-26.

Reese, Jean A. "Comparison and Evaluation of Three CD-ROM Products." *Optical Information Systems '87 Proceedings,* December 1-3, 1987, New York Hilton Hotel. Meckler Corporation, Westport, CT.

"Review and Commentary on the Working Paper for Information Processing: Volume and File Structure of CD-ROM For Information Interchange." *Optical Information Systems* 7:1 (January/February 1987): 50-56. Meckler Corporation, Westport, CT.

Ropiequet, Suzanne. *CD-ROM: The New Papyrus.* Redmond, WA: Microsoft Press, 1986.

———, et al. *CD-ROM: Optical Publishing.* Redmond, WA: Microsoft Publishing, 1987.

Roth, Judith Paris. *The Essential Guide to CD-ROM.* Westport, CT: Meckler Corporation, 1986.

Schaub, John A. "CD-ROM for Public Access Catalogs." *Library Hi Tech* 11 (1986): 7-13.

Schwerin, Julie B. *CD-ROM Standards: The Book*. Published jointly by Learned Information, Oxford, UK; InfoTech, Pittsfield, VT.

Shain, Kenneth S. "Graphic Environment Operations for CD-ROM." *Optical Information Systems* 6:6 (September/October 1986): 399-402. Meckler Corporation, Westport, CT.

Snow, Bonnie. "Med-Base: Ease of Use and Search Accuracy." *ONLINE* (May 1987): 125-133. Online, Inc., Weston, CT.

Special Issue on CD-ROM Technology in Libraries. *Optical Information Systems* 7:6 (November/December 1987). Meckler Corporation, Westport, CT.

Spiter, Gerald A. *The Disconnection: Interactive Video and Optical Disc Media*. White Plains, NY: Knowledge Industry Publications, Inc., 1987.

Strukhoff, Roger. "The Industry Emerges: Apple Shines in Seattle." *CD-ROM Review* (May 1988): 12-16.

Tiampo, Janet. "Update on Retrieval Software Products." *Optical Information Systems '87 Proceedings*, December 1-3, 1987, New York Hilton Hotel. Meckler Corporation, Westport, CT.

"Working Paper for Information Processing: Volume and File Structure of CD-ROM for Information Interchange." *Optical Information Systems* 7:1 (January/February 1987): 29-49. Meckler Corporation, Westport, CT.

General Reading Resources

CD Data Report. Published by Diversified Data Resources, Inc., Falls Church, VA.

CD-ROM Librarian. Published by Meckler Corporation, Westport, CT.

CD-ROM Review. Published by CW Communications, Peterborough, NH.

Optical Information Systems Magazine. Published by Meckler Corporation, Westport, CT.

Optical Information Systems Update. Published by Meckler Corporation, Westport, CT.

Understanding Computers: Memory and Storage. Time-Life Books, Alexandria, VA.

Index

This index consists primarily of the names of companies, organizations, and products mentioned in this book.

Contributors

Norman Desmarais, acquisitions librarian at Providence College in Rhode Island, has written extensively on CD-ROM technology in *Byte, Advances in Librarianship, Library Software Review,* and *Electronic and Optical Publishing Review.* He is author of *The Librarian's CD-ROM Handbook,* contributing editor to *Optical Information Systems,* and a member of the advisory board of *CD-ROM Librarian.*

Sandra Helsel, Ph.D., is an educational consultant and writer specializing in interactive curriculum. Her firm, Interactive Learning, Ltd., focuses on the application and utilization of interactive technologies including CD-I, CD-ROM, and interactive videodisc in various educational environments.

Nancy Melin Nelson is founder and editor of *CD-ROM Librarian,* editor of *Small Computers in Libraries,* author of *Library Applications of Optical Disk and CD-ROM Technology,* and contributing editor to *CD-ROM Review* and *Optical Information Systems.* She is a specialist in library applications of emerging technologies, and consults for companies interested in this special market niche.

Patti Myers provides consulting in the marketing of publishing services, and in the application of new technologies in publishing and information processes. She is the author of *Publishing with CD-ROM: A Guide to Compact Disc Optical Storage Technologies for Providers of Publishing Services,* published by Meckler Corporation in 1987.

Mary Ann O'Connor, president of Compact Discoveries, Inc., is editor, Compact Disc Technologies, *Optical Information Systems Update.* Compact Discoveries is a computer applications development firm specializing in optical disk technology and has been involved in the design of several read-only optical disk application products.

Judith Paris Roth, editor of *Optical Information Systems* magazine and chairperson of the annual OIS Conference and Exposition sponsored by Meckler Corporation, has been actively involved with read-only and write-once optical disc technology since 1980. Author of the *Essential Guide to CD-ROM,* she has written extensively about optical storage technology in *Popular Computing, Journal of the American Society for Information Science, High Technology, Library Software Review, AAP Newsletter,* and *Educational and Instructional Television.*